The Window
of Vulnerability

The Window of Vulnerability

A POLITICAL SPIRITUALITY

Dorothee Soelle
Translated by Linda M. Maloney

FORTRESS PRESS   **MINNEAPOLIS**

For Luise

THE WINDOW OF VULNERABILITY
A Political Spirituality

First English-language edition published 1990 by Fortress Press.

Cover design: Eric Walljasper
Internal design: Karen Buck
Author photo: Joanna Roy

Library of Congress Cataloging-in-Publication Data

Sölle, Dorothee.
   [Fenster der Verwundbarkeit. English. Selections]
   The window of vulnerability : a political spirituality / Dorothee
Soelle : translated by Linda M. Maloney.
     p.   cm.
   Translation of selections from: Das Fenster der Verwundbarkeit.
   Includes bibliographical references.
   ISBN 0-8006-2432-7 (alk. paper)
   1. Christianity and politics.   2. Peace—Religious aspects—
Christianity.   3. Feminist theology.   4. Liberation theology.
I. Title.
BR115.P7S61213   1990
261.7—dc20   90-35406
                                                       CIP

Maufactured in the U.S.A.   AF 1–2432

94   93   92   91   90   1   2   3   4   5   6   7   8   9   10

Contents

The Window of Vulnerability

The window of vulnerability
must be closed—
so the military say
to justify the arms race

My skin
is a window of vulnerability
without moisture, without touching
I must die

The window of vulnerability
is being walled up
my land
cannot live

We need light
so we can think
we need air
so we can breathe
we need a window
open toward heaven.

Preface

At a certain stage in the development of cancer, although it is not impossible to locate the metastases of the disease, it makes less and less sense to do so. The metastases have spread and have invaded the organs that were not previously affected. They have taken over the whole body. The organs that were not attacked at first now begin to reduce their functions, or they work on behalf of the disease: they grow. For cancer is not a reduction, a wasting, a deficiency disease, but rather an excess, an unbridled growth in which the distinction between origin and metastases becomes pointless. The present book can be read in light of the questions, What stage of the disease have we now reached? Which of the organs of society are still free of cancer? How deep has militarization penetrated? Are there still windows in the ultimate bunker?

It was in the context of the debate over mobile intercontinental ballistic missiles that I first heard the military strategists speak of a "window of vulnerability." It was their term for a gap in the defense system, a possible spot where an enemy could break through. There were two articles in the *New York Times,* one for and one against, in which two political commentators discussed whether the MX missiles could really close this "window of vulnerability." One said yes, at least partially; the other said the solution was inadequate. There was no disagreement about whether this window had to be closed or not. Both writers agreed on that goal; they did not even raise the question.

It then occurred to me how far advanced the militarization of our minds is. Apparently no one is aware that the window of vulnerability has to remain open—that is, as long as we human beings exist or want to go on doing so. It is as if we were doing our utmost to shield ourselves from the light. Certainly, every window makes us vulnerable and is a sign of relationship, receptivity, communication—which are, in various forms, the subjects of this book. The window opens toward a peace that would not begin to occur to the *Times* experts.

The window of vulnerability is a window toward heaven. It is the whole aim of this book to open that window as wide as possible. The book contains texts from the past eight years. If I were to name dates that define this period for me, I would begin with December 12, 1979, and the catastrophic NATO decision to escalate the arms race, and I would end with Heinrich Böll's death on July 16, 1985. In these years of struggle it became more and more important to reflect on that which carries and sustains us. In a certain sense I have become more conservative: in my trust in the tradition, in my progressively deepening rootedness in the Jewish and Christian heritage. Daniel Berrigan, in conversation, compared the church of Jesus Christ to an umbrella: It is not always where we are, but it follows and protects us. The tradition does not let us stand alone in the cold rain.

I say this consciously as a woman who is seeking to appropriate the tradition in its humanistic form—that is, in those features that are supportive of women, without denying its sexist and even misogynist characteristics: God, for me, is not simply a symbol of patriarchy.

The resistance that has grown in my country during these years has deep roots in the tradition, and it is certain that this tradition helps me to see the White Rose that bloomed in Munich in the years of 1942–43 blooming here and now as well. Now, as always, I see it as my task to do liberation theology for the people of the First World and to articulate the culture in which I live from that perspective.

I feel a need to explain to the American reader a certain shift of hope that I experienced with the beginning of the eighties. Crossing the Atlantic in order to teach at Union Theological Seminary, New York, since 1975 I had understood part of my work to build bridges between the new and the old world. I gathered information and picked up new ideas, trends, books, films, and theologies as well. My mind was enormously stretched and I tried to communicate as much as possible from the intellectual and spiritual wealth I found in the new world. Yet in the early eighties my needs changed.

Getting more deeply involved in the European resistance movement of Christian greens, feminists, and ecopacifists, my role slowly changed: instead of bringing back home the fresh insights from the center of the new world I started to import things to it, to my friends, students, and readers. I do not think that our current struggles and our dreams of "a country in which it would be easier to be good," as one of my North American heroines, Dorothy Day, put it, are so much different. But my sense of hope and the capacity of changing the apocalyptic tendency of the one world we share are more rooted by now in the European context. The peace movement that represents the context of many of the texts in this book is one case in point. Will the minorities of faith among whom I live continue to increase on both sides of the Atlantic? Will God become more visible among ourselves? Will we keep the window of vulnerability open?

In German mythology, Siegfried is the most powerful hero. He kills a dragon and bathes in the monster's hot blood. This bath gives him a horny skin no sword can penetrate; he becomes invulnerable. What is the dream behind this myth? It is a male fantasy, to be the strongest and at the same time to be invulnerable. Dragon's blood is the sacramental sign of the powerful. They have bathed in it, these impervious beings with their victors' smiles. They want to wall up all the windows. No light is to peek in; nothing must ever touch them. Transcendence is dangerous because it makes us vulnerable. Therefore the state, which has raised up the idol of invulnerability in the name of "security," must attempt to disallow all genuine transcendence; only the false transcendence that has reduced itself to the otherworldly and the individual is allowed. Many of the church conflicts of recent years have revealed this either-or, this "either Caesar or Christ." The masculine myth of the invulnerable hero is opposed to the unarmed carpenter's son from Galilee: there is nothing here to harmonize.

That transcendence creates vulnerability is true for all religions, but in Christianity it is driven to the limit: in Christ, God makes Godself vulnerable; in Christ, God defines God as nonviolent. The manly ideal of invulnerability is opposed, in fact caricatured, by the Crucified, who was and is experienced by his friends as Son of God. And if we really understand the parable of the last judgment, in which every hungry child is Christ (Matthew 25), we can say: Christ is God's wound in the world. Therefore we need a window of vulnerability if we want to live in inward relationship with Christ. There are still churches that mix the Blood of the Lamb with dragon's blood. They try to subject us to this world's dominant ideals of invulnerability and success, and in so doing they close the window of vulnerability. But it is the only window toward heaven that we have. That is exactly what Martin Luther was after in trying to develop a theology of the cross; that tradition is not in search of *securitas*, security in the dragon's blood, but of *certitudo,* certainty in the one who was most vulnerable of all.

I dedicate this book to my "best friend," to use a child's expression. Luise Schottroff, New Testament scholar, has helped me to learn to read the Bible with exactitude and enthusiasm; to rescue it from the "Bible thieves" of whom Thomas Müntzer spoke long ago; and especially to put it to use. My best friend laughs with me when men strut around like arrogant roosters; she weeps with me when the fish die in the Rhine. Her Prussian realism casts a gently indignant eye over my mystical flights, and my Rhineland optimism teases her suspiciousness. Her tenacious constancy has rooted me anew, again and again, in this Motherland of ours.

Dorothee Soelle
Hamburg

PART ONE
Security Is Death

No animal eats another of its own species for
the pleasure of it; no animal kills its own kind
in cold blood at someone else's order.
—J. G. Herder

We Want Peace,
Not Security

Human beings are defenseless creatures. Without tusks or fangs, without pelt or bristles, needing more care and protection than other animals, they enter the world, biologically one year too soon. They need the society of others. Their lack of armor or other protection impels them to make tools in order to survive: the human is the "tool-making animal." But perhaps we ought to update the traditional formula, since the majority of tools and the mass of technology that are being made nowadays by men (who imagine themselves to be "man") are directed not to survival, but to destruction, to "overkill."

What is behind this organized will to murder "at someone else's order" (a general, a parliament, a weapons manufacturer) "in cold blood" (without responsibility, without any personal interest translated into the deed) that determines our scientific, economic, and ideological reality? It is the urge of the defenseless animal to protect itself. But today we need peace, not security.

"There is no way to peace," said Mahatma Gandhi. "Peace is the way." This statement is one of the many thought-provoking slogans of the peace movement that, in gratifying contrast to the triviality of most official political slogans, should be read as signaling the beginning of an alternative political culture. As simple as it sounds, this statement calls into question one of the most important truisms of our political thought, namely, the distinction between means and ends. If the end is good, the means may be ugly, violent, costly, and unreasonable; the higher end "sanctifies" them. In almost every discussion about peace, I hear the statement that of course we all want peace; we simply have different ideas about the right way to achieve it. No, I reply, not everybody wants peace. The Reagan administration, for example, didn't want the peace that we in the peace movement

3

are seeking. No, the possession of more opportunities for overkill is not the way to peace. No, the goal of peace does not sanctify the means of extermination; the truth is that when the means are absolutely contrary to the end, they devour it.

The means-end relationship must, at the very least, express an adaptation of the means to the end, and the goal, while viewed in a particular time frame, must always remain present and visible. The continual delaying of the goal to a later time ("We will disarm when we have acquired sufficient armaments to allow us to negotiate from a position of strength") is destructive of the goal itself. In this delay, the "now" of peace that is the basis of Gandhi's thought is denied. The idea of finding "a way to peace" that in itself is not peaceful is counterproductive. Peace is the way to peace, and if the way and the goal, the means and the end, contradict one another, as the strategy of deterrence demands, the goal undergoes a change that at first is not noticed by many who "want peace, of course." This process is clear enough to the cynics of power; they are concerned with "security." Their concept of peace has no content beyond the safeguarding of their interests. One of the many ways that language has been warped in recent years, as predicted by George Orwell, is the destruction of the word *peace* by government propaganda, which nowadays usually attaches to *peace* the words *and freedom*; peace is not allowed to run around naked and unattended anymore.

The confusion of peace with security is a daily routine in our violent state of affairs. Judicial peace, school peace, marital peace—all degenerate into security under the influence of violent methods. The use of violence, expressed in force, extortion, and control, destroys the end and increasingly replaces it with violence itself as the only goal. Thus security, which we are supposed to receive in exchange when we forgo genuine peace, is increasingly neuroticized: our need for it becomes insatiable; one can never be secure enough. When a woman is unsure of her partner and constantly telephones to check up on him, she has already traded what she perhaps still thinks of as love for the security she needs. Her desire for a completely controllable relationship is neurotic. To paraphrase Gandhi, there is no "way to love," for love is the way.

In the search for controllable security, peace still seems to be a desired goal, but in fact it has faded to propaganda that is fed to a particular audience. The secondary value, security, has absorbed the primary value, peace; the person capable of peace is replaced by an armed one, and that is precisely what the bourgeoisie now think of when they think of peace: security. They were disgusted by the rhetorical blunders of the Reagan administration, by the talk of limited and winnable atomic war. Between imperialism, which seeks world domination, if only the "evil empire" and the "focus of evil in the modern world" can first be eliminated, and genuine peace built on justice, which in practice implies an option for the poor, the middle class has chosen a third way: securing the situation in which we live, a situation that has been the same thing as war for a long time now, at least for the fifteen thousand people who, according to the most conservative estimates, fall victim to it every day.

When I speak of genuine peace, I mean the reconciliation of the partners in conflict, not their militarization; I mean more justice in trade relationships between poor and rich. To postpone the need for peace as articulated by the biblical prophets altogether to the end of time is to twist the longing of all peoples and to destroy oneself: as if peace could only be had at the beginning of the ages. That the lion and the lamb feed together has a thoroughly concrete and present meaning—or is it too much to ask that we imagine the United States and the inhabitants of Pacific islands fishing beside one another? Is it really illusionary to let the little child play by the adder's den and to suppose that an American government could permit the Sandinista experiment on its doorstep?

The great majority of citizens of the First World have, in fact, abandoned such goals as utopian and make do, under the name of security, with prevention of the worst—which, of course, means only the worst for *them*. "Security" is hope reduced to middle-class terms, yearning on a small scale, a kind of self-limitation that already amounts to mutilation.

The bourgeoisie make a business of whatever they do. Even their concept of peace is shaped by the spirit of *do ut des* (I give so that you will give). The peace negotiators who travel to Geneva or Stockholm are men who act like business agents. They receive good evaluations if they gain a lot and pay little, if they manage to dismantle many enemy weapons and bring them home, so to speak, as booty, while at the same time they give up as few as possible of their own tools of mass murder. The arms control negotiations rest on this understanding of business, of contract. For the negotiators, peace is a business—good when it is successful and promises satisfaction to both sides.

In this sense the concept of bilateralism is one that does not surpass the moral level of the bourgeoisie. The central value, security, may not be encroached upon in the name of peace. But just as, in Gandhi's mind, there could be no "way to peace" that was different from peace itself, so it is impossible that a business deal should bring about an increase in peace. The concept of bilateralism, the idea that both superpowers could scale themselves down again, has lost its credibility after thirty-five years of escalation of armaments. It has not worked and it will not work. If peace is a business like any other, perhaps we ought to bury our vision of peace altogether and content ourselves with managing the security neurosis. Armed people have no peace.

What I have learned about this in recent years could be described as the step from bilateralism to unilateralism. I think that, up to December 12, 1979, the day of the decision that has had such serious consequences for Europe [namely, to station medium-range missiles there], I was an unconscious bilateralist. I thought that negotiations, rational discussion, agreements, contracts, *do ut des*, could bring us closer to peace. The European peace movement, especially the Dutch, who worked out this question very early, opened my eyes to the fact that this liberal hope is a middle-class illusion, a rational superficiality, a narrowing of our desire for peace to a bourgeois need to be secure. Within this security syndrome we no longer act politically; we only react, but without breaking the circle of violence. We supposedly arm "to catch up," but really "to stay ahead," and the need for security, separated from peace, its true goal, continues to swell like a cancerous growth.

But just as it is not possible, in personal conflicts between two people, to bring about basic changes through agreements, contracts, and business deals, so also in political relationships the bourgeois reduction of rational dealing to the level of business is not very promising. This type of prudent dealing has stagnated for long enough. It is not getting us anywhere. It argues that what people need is not real peace, but simply security. But "where there is no prophecy, the people cast off restraint" (Prov. 29:18). If we exchange the vision of peace for the supposed security of escalating armaments and continue on the present course of creating a fortress bristling with weaponry, we will make our country more and more unlivable. The vision of peace and disarmament can only be one-sided. All the historical experience of the last thirty years speaks against the hope that we could achieve a limitation of this madness by means of bilateral negotiations. An appropriate vision for the European people today would be to do without the protection of atomic weapons and so to break out of the circle of violence. Unilateralism is a necessary precondition for this new vision. To think unilaterally means to recognize that insanity is not reason, not even when it is mutual and by agreement.

If we really want peace, we must begin disarming where we are—on one side, which is neither better nor worse than the other side, but has the advantage of being *our* side. It is rationalistic stupidity to suppose that mutual death threats can be abolished from the world through a kind of business deal. Both partners give a little, and then we have a nice balance again. Those are deceptive hopes, nourished by the idea of security and constituting a betrayal of any real hope of peace. Change can only happen when one of the partners to the conflict begins to relinquish his or her threatening attitude and makes a tiny step forward alone. Unilateralism contains an existential moment when the rationalism of business sense is abandoned. Change happens at the level of action that contains risk.

The illusion of bourgeois concepts of security lies, I think, in the expectation that peace can come from business dealings, from rational agreement. Behind this idea lies a rationalistic optimism that flies in the face of the genuine despair of peoples subjected to the ideology of security. The history of religions—I include here the history of the nonviolent martyrs like Martin Luther King, Steve Biko, and Oscar Romero—teaches a very different lesson. It says: It doesn't happen without victims. It doesn't happen without risk. Life that excludes and protects itself against death protects itself to death. If the "window of vulnerability," as it is called in military language, is finally closed and walled up, the supposedly secure people inside the fortress will die for lack of light and air. Only life that opens itself to the other, life that risks being wounded or killed, contains promise. Those who arm themselves are not only killers; they are already dead.

One of the U.S. peace movement's posters shows a kind of altar standing in a desert landscape. The altar is built on three steps. On top of it stands a bomb, with its nose pointing to the skies; people kneel around it in adoration. The scene is a copy of the biblical story of the golden calf: the bomb is the golden calf from whom the people beg security.

The Reformers' tradition teaches that people always have some kind of god because there is always something they "fear and love above all things."[1] Even atheists have a god in this sense, to whom they bring sacrifices, for whom they work, and from whom they expect security. The correct theological question is thus not whether someone lives with or without a god, but rather which god is worshiped and adored in a particular society. Under the sign of global militarization, as it is now being practiced in and from the Western world, the God-question is easily answered: The god of "this world" is the bomb.

The bomb as symbol has a variety of meanings, on different levels of relevance for our culture. It has an economic meaning, especially evident in the analysis of the connection between militarization and underdevelopment. At the request of the United Nations, a study was prepared showing the negative consequences of armaments for the developing nations. This research report, completed for the 1982 special session of the UN on disarmament, treated the interconnection of weapons, development, and global security. The document is often referred to as the Thorsson Report, after Inge Thorsson, who directed the research. It considers how financial resources, raw materials, energy, and human work are put to use for military purposes. The balance of the report, in light of the never-ending demands of the military sector, is devastating. Appended to the report is a list of products needed by the developing nations in those sectors necessary to sustain life: agriculture, production and distribution of energy, medicine, transportation, and the like. All these products could be manufactured and effect real changes in those countries if military industry were converted to peaceful purposes.

The calf in Israel's history was made of gold. It was a symbol of security and welfare. As the calf was forged from the people's jewelry and ornaments, the Israelites said: "This is your God, O Israel, who brought you up out of the land of Egypt" (Exod. 32:4). When I listen to the courtly speeches of West German politicians, I hear them saying exactly the same thing: It is the bomb that protects us from the Communists and brings us prosperity, security, and power. Whoever wants to retain prosperity and security must adore the bomb and must fear, love, and trust it above all things.

The bomb as symbol has another meaning in the field of science. In 1980, 42 percent of all scientists and engineers in the United States were doing military work. In their research and development of new means of mass destruction they are, often without knowing it, adoring the bomb. On a world scale, the majority of all individual projects in scientific research and technological development are devoted to military purposes. That also means that the majority of scientists and technicians, immersed in their adoration of the bomb, are completely out of touch with reality. Millions of people lack both clean water and the technologies to make water usable. Millions are without shelter and have no technical means for making houses out of the local raw materials. Millions are starving and have not learned how to produce nourishing food where they live. But science, untouched by the real suffering of humanity, persists in its fascination with death and seeks to create more and better instruments for killing.

The bomb-symbol also has sexual significance, and not only because of its shape. In patriarchal culture, the man's sexual potency is thought to be connected not only with happiness, but also with violence. The German word *Vergewaltigung* for rape (*Gewalt* means force or violence) clearly expresses the fact that men can experience sex as violence, conquest, humiliation, and degradation of other persons. The golden calf was, from its origins in the Canaanite cult, really a golden steer. The adoration of the bomb is adoration of violence in every form.

The women's movement has repeatedly uncovered the connections between male dominance and war, between maleness and self-identification with the warrior, between lust and violence. The adoration of bombs made by men is only logical in this sense: In a culture that defines the human as a man and makes of woman an unknown, publicly invisible, irrelevant being, the bomb, which is the ultimate weapon, must necessarily become the most important cultural symbol. Just as the desire for security does not rise above the moral level of the bourgeoisie, so also the political culture of the present, whose heart and soul are fixed on the bomb, cannot surpass the level of the men who are its rulers. The bomb prohibits any kind of transcendence. It is God, the final, unquestionable reality. The precedence that so-called defense takes over all other political interests makes that quite obvious. In the day-to-day speeches of politicians who serve the military we can clearly hear the refrain: "You shall have no other gods besides me." Defense takes absolute precedence before all other political and social priorities.

In this sense the symbol of the bomb has religious meaning. If I am correct in my observation that political conflicts are becoming more and more obviously religious, that they more and more clearly express absolutely different world views, that they are less and less capable of being liberally smoothed over and rationalized, then the bomb is in fact the god of "this world." The people who adore the bomb carry it within themselves and feel themselves secure in its shadow.

In Toronto, Canada, there is a Center for Culture and Technology that collects and continues the work of philosopher and communications theorist Marshall McLuhan, who died in 1980. Dr. Derrick de Kerckhove, director of the McLuhan Program, recently expressed the idea that the atomic bomb, considered as a medium of information, was a good thing. He said in support of the stationing of new nuclear missiles in Europe: "I'm absolutely delighted the bomb is there. It's about time we had something to bring us together." The essential thought of this successor of McLuhan was that the bomb is a modern myth holding power over the culture's thinking similar to that formerly possessed by religion. "That myth has become a physical part of everyone's brain and is now acting as a strong unifying force." The bomb is "the ultimate information medium . . . the more bombs the better!" De Kerckhove "is sorry that [Pershing II and Cruise missiles] are not widely distributed in public places, such as markets." The bomb is a universal myth; "it . . . binds people together in a way they have not been linked since the Middle Ages."[2] It is clear that, as far as McLuhan's successor is concerned, the bomb will not be used. Disarmament is therefore unnecessary. The medium is the message.

I mention this because I consider it more than intellectual nonsense. It is in fact the intellectual and scientific expression of the religion that militarism is propagating on earth. The real, practical adoration of the bomb has found its ideology. One characteristic of this religion is that it cannot distinguish God from Satan. That is also true of the fundamentalists who predict the end of the world as God's will and promote it through their politics. God, for them, is neither love nor justice, but pure power. Militarization of the whole world is the accomplishment of this God: strength is his highest ideal, violence his method, and security his promise.

The peace movement has freed itself from this god. That liberation involves a "conversion": turning away from false life, turning toward another form of life. In recent years I have again and again met people who have told me, with tears in their eyes, that they have only been "involved" in the peace movement for a few months, and that it has changed their whole lives. "Now I know why I am here." Those are the conversions that are happening, in huge numbers, before our eyes: the turning from a violent society to a peaceful one in which conflicts are carried through bloodlessly and without weapons. The image the Bible uses for this conversion is drawn entirely from materials and technology. It does not speak simply of a change of heart, but rather of a conversion of the armaments industry to a peaceful industry: swords into plowshares.

Thanks to the massive disruption, or rather destruction, of religion by the dominant churches in our country, many people do not even know that the conversion from security to peace is the most important religious event in their lives—just as our bishops fail to comprehend that people are seeking God when they fasten stickers proclaiming "Fight Atomic Death" on the doors of their houses. When they do this, they have converted the bourgeois desire for security, mediated by possessions and property, into the universal longing for peace, a desire that includes the other members of the human family as well and that is mediated by another way of being, namely, being for others.

This is only a start. Someday this movement will be so strong, so unmistakable, so ready to renounce and to suffer, that everyone will be able to see the other God within it. Today it is plain that whoever continues to arm some people is working toward the death of all. Why did God make us as weaponless beings in the first place? The movement to disarm the human being is just beginning.

Notes

1. Martin Luther, *Small Catechism*.
2. *New York Times*, 12 February 1984, 20.

Life to the Full

SPEECH TO THE GENERAL ASSEMBLY
OF THE WORLD COUNCIL OF CHURCHES
IN VANCOUVER, CANADA, 1983

Sisters and brothers,
I am speaking to you as a woman who comes from one of the richest countries on earth; a land with a bloody history smelling of gas, which some of us Germans have not been able to forget; a land that today contains the thickest concentration of nuclear weapons on earth. I want to say something to you about the fear that reigns in my comfortable, militaristic country. I speak to you in rage, in censure, and in sorrow. This grief concerning my country, this friction with my society, is not a matter of caprice and has not come about because I had nothing better to do. Rather, it is rooted in my faith in the life of the world, encountered in the poor man from Nazareth who had neither riches nor weapons. This poor man places the life of the world before our eyes and points us toward the ground of all life, toward God. Christ is the exegesis of God, the interpretation who makes us understand who God is (John 1:18).

I do not mean that in the sense of a religious imperialism, as if there were no other interpretations of God in other religions, but rather in the sense of an unconditional duty to get involved with Jesus Christ if we seek the life of the world and not its death.

Christ came into the world in order that all people "might have life and have it to the full," or, in another translation, so that "they might live and have abundance of all they need" (John 10:10). What is this "life to the full"? Where does it happen? Who lives it? I see two ways in which it is destroyed in our world: *poverty without* and *emptiness within*.

For about two-thirds of the human family there is no "life to the full," because they live in poverty, in naked, economically caused impoverishment on the brink of death. They are hungry, they have no homes, they have no schools or medicine for their children, no pure water to drink, no work—and they do not know how to get free of their oppressors. Trade agreements and international relationships are imposed on the poor by the first, rich world; the poor plunge farther and farther into a misery that increases day by day. The struggle for survival destroys the fulfilled life, God's *shalom* of which the Bible speaks, in which people need not worry about daily nourishment, where they are healthy, are not menaced by enemies, and enjoy a long life in family and community. "Long life is in her right hand; in her left hand are riches and honor," as it says in Proverbs (3:16). Poverty destroys this life promised to all people.

Here I want to read you a letter from a Brazilian woman, dictated to a nun because the woman herself cannot write:

> I, Severina, come from the northeast. There, in my land, two of my babies died because I had no milk. On one day in my village I saw forty-two little coffins carried to the cemetery. My sister-in-law, who was very poor, had borne seventeen children: three of them lived; all the others died between the ages of one and four years. Two of the three surviving children are not normal. I was with her when she delivered, and sometimes we didn't even have a piece of fresh linen in which to wrap the baby. It is the same with many families, thousands of them: ten or fifteen children, and five or six out of ten die. There really are priests who tell us: "You are lucky if you have seven children who die very young: a circle of angels is waiting for you in heaven." But who really knows what it means for a woman to wait nine months for a child, ten times or maybe even more, weeping all the time during the first three months because she won't be able to raise the child? Are you supposed to love it, and see it starve after four months?
>
> Is that really what they mean when they talk about "human dignity"? I see that Christ in the gospel, which Claudio and Vera often read to me, really loved poverty; but he couldn't stand people's suffering. There is a difference between being poor and not being able to give one's baby anything more than sugar water, and you give it water and know that it will die.

Christ came so that all might "have life to the full," but the absolute poverty that is a crime in a technologically developed world destroys people physically, spiritually, psychically, and also religiously, because it poisons hope and caricatures faith, turning it into powerless apathy. Exploitation, the sin of the rich, intrudes between Christ, who means the fullness of life for all, and the poor, as it attempts to destroy Christ's promise. In John's Gospel, Christ says, in connection with this "fullness of life": "I am the door; the one who enters by me will be saved, and will go in and out and find pasture. The thief comes only to steal and kill and destroy; I came that they may have life and have it abundantly" (10:9-10).

Christ and "the thief" are contrasted to one another. The thief comes to plunder the poor, so that they will die. Christ has come to bring the fullness of life. But it would be a childish kind of Christianity simply to wait and see whether the thief or Christ comes to us. We are participants in one of these two projects: exploitation or fullness of life. We either participate in the mission of Christ or in the thief's plan for the world. As long as we are only victims or spectators of this struggle for justice, we support the thief and his crime. In the struggle for a more just world, on the other hand, we participate in God's plan of creation that has entrusted the world to us so that it may yield fullness of life for all.

Fullness of life is impossible in absolute, compulsory poverty. But even in the rich First World there is little fulfilled life; instead, there is a growing inner emptiness. It is not material pauperization but psychic emptiness that intrudes itself between Christ and the middle classes of the First World. Life without meaning, sensed by many sensitive individuals since the beginning of industrialization, is today the experience of masses of people in the First World. Nothing gives joy, nothing hurts deeply, relationships to others are superficial and interchangeable, hopes and desires extend only as far as next year's summer vacation. Most people's work is unsatisfying, senseless, and boring. We were made by God to be men and women capable of work and of love. In our work and in our sexuality, in the broadest sense of the word, we share in creation; fullness of life also means becoming a working and loving human being. But the lives of most people in the First World resemble instead an extended death that can last many years.

This death is painless; there are enough pills, after all. It is unfeeling: "Don't be so emotional!" is a harsh criticism in our language. It is pitiless, because life is seen as self-made and not as the gift of the

Creator. It is a soulless life in a world where everything is reckoned according to exchange value. Nothing is beautiful in itself, nothing promises joy in and of itself; all that matters is what you can get for it. We are empty and at the same time sated with superfluous goods and wares. There is a peculiar relationship between the many things we possess and consume and the emptiness of our real existence. If Christ came that we might have fullness of life, capitalism has come to turn everything into money. That is the extended death we see in blank and empty faces. Think of a traffic jam: Each driver sits alone in his or her tin box and pushes him- or herself slowly but aggressively forward. Frustration and hate directed to those before and behind are quite normal. That is an image of the emptiness of life in the rich world.

In the gospel we find the story of the rich young man who apparently has fullness of life as represented by many possessions and who nevertheless is overcome by the inner emptiness of his life. He is doing well. He has what he needs and much more. But he searches beyond possession and contentment: What shall I do with my life? What can I do to make my life more unambiguous, more radical, less splintered, uncompromised? How can I escape from the half-heartedness of my existence?

I saw a letter that could have come from the rich young man's brother. This man, a normal member of the white European middle class, writes:

> I am thirty-five years old, a civil servant with a good job, married. We have two children. Our marriage is harmonious thus far. The children are doing well. I have everything I need, a secure and well-paid profession, everything fine at home. But lately I feel uneasy, in spite of everything. I feel more and more that my life is empty. I lack something, but I don't know what. Sometimes I think I ought to throw away everything and just take off. But I haven't the strength to do it. You can't just give up everything you have put together. . . . What shall I do?

I see these two faces before me, the West German civil servant and the rich young man in the New Testament. They have everything they need, and still they lack everything. They are not hard, masculine, successful types; they are not brutal, but soft. They did not achieve their positions and their wealth by killing and stealing, by calumniating others, tricking or cheating them. They probably take care of their parents and do not mistreat their wives. They are polite and disinclined to any kind of radicalism. Both of them want something from their lives: They want to gain everlasting life. They want to be whole, to live complete and undivided lives and to reflect something of the beauty of fullness. But their lives have no sparkle. They don't shine. The surface, instead, is empty, and behind it lurks long-drawn-out death.

The evangelist Mark says that Jesus looked at the rich young man and loved him (10:21). Jesus wants to entice him and all of us to more life than we have yet had. This rich young man, too, could come to fullness of life. He even knows that he lacks something, that he can expect more from life. And yet there is something fundamentally false about his idea of eternal life. He thinks: I have everything, and I have kept all the rules. Only one thing is lacking—the meaning of life, its fulfillment. If that can be added to the rest, everything will be well.

Jesus reverses this expectation: The young man has too much, not too little. "Sell what you have, and give to the poor, and you will have treasure in heaven; and come, follow me" (Mark 10:21).

Many middle-class people are seeking today for a new spirituality. They want to add something to what they already have: education and profession, upbringing and secure income, family and friends. Religious fulfillment, the meaning of life, food for the soul, consolation—all that is to be added on top of material security, as a kind of religious surplus for those who are already overprivileged. They seek spiritual fulfillment of life in addition to the material blessing from above to supplement their riches.

But Jesus rejects this pious middle-class hope. Fullness of life does not come when you already have everything. You have to become empty for God's fullness. Give away what you have; give it to the poor. Then you will have found what you are seeking. The story of the rich young man ends in sorrow: Jesus' words sadden the young man, and he goes away. Maybe he will succumb to depression, maybe he will soon begin to drink, maybe he will cause an automobile accident. He did not let himself be enticed by Jesus to fullness of life, to sharing of life.

On the walls of many houses in West Germany is written the English phrase No Future. The people who feel this way are young and vital. They cannot imagine bringing a child into this world, and they plant no more trees. Life to the full, Christ's promise, brings only a weary smile to their faces. Their sorrow is sometimes directed aggressively outward and sometimes depressively inward. Their lives are empty.

Jesus, too, goes away sorrowing in this story. "How hard it is for the rich to enter the reign of God!" (Mark 10:23). Fullness of life, the reign of God, eternal life—all shatter before wealth of possessions, exploitation, and injustice. But the rich young man doesn't even know that. His life is a hopeless sorrow and a sorrowful hopelessness. Why are so many people in the rich world so empty? Excess things make life itself excessive. There is a strong desire, precisely in the younger generation, to become independent of ownership of too many things. Henry David Thoreau said: "The opportunities of living are diminished in proportion as what are called the 'means' are increased. The best thing a man can do for his culture when he is rich is to endeavour to carry out those schemes which he entertained when he was poor."[1] The economy alone cannot explain this emptiness: They have everything, we say, what can they possibly want? I doubt, too, that individual psychology, that opium of the middle class, can explain anything of this; I do not believe that we need to know the rich young man's parents and analyze their relationship with their son before we can understand the story of his life with God. I think what we really need is a knowledge of God—theology—in order to understand the empty and senseless life of the rich.

God is the ground and basis of life: God breathed the breath of life into humanity (Gen. 2:7). If we hide from God behind our wealth of possessions so that God cannot touch us, we die—the long-drawn-out death of the middle class that also touches the elites of the Third World. Wealth functions like a wall, much more impenetrable than the famous Berlin wall. We keep ourselves apart, we make ourselves untouchable; our wall is soundproof, so that we cannot hear the cries of the poor and oppressed. Apartheid is not merely a political system in one country in Africa; apartheid is a particular way of thinking, feeling, and living without consciousness of what is going on all around us. There is a way of doing theology without ever letting the poor and economically exploited become visible or audible—that is apartheid theology. I am speaking of my own social class now, but I want to include all those in other economic circumstances who follow the same ideals, even if they have not yet achieved them.

Dear sisters and brothers from the Third and Second World, I beg you: Do not follow us! Demand the return of what we have stolen from you, but do not follow us. If you do, you will have to bid a sorrowful farewell to Christ as did the rich young man. Do not accept the notion of "fullness of life" that we have developed in the Western world. It is a lie. It separates us from God. It makes us rich and dead.

The psychic emptiness of the rich is a consequence of the economic injustice from which they profit. We have chosen a system built on money and violence. The rich youth will fall victim to depression. He cannot change anything in his life, he can only make it secure. He will have to make it more and more secure so that no one can take anything from him; therefore he piles up weapons. The gentle depressiveness of so many European and North American churches is their practical acceptance of militarism. They have no hope because they trust in the death-dealing peace of those who build up arms. Money and violence go together: Those who have made money their god must make security their national ideology and armaments their political priority.

Many Christians in our countries say: What is so terrible about making ourselves secure through armaments? We don't want to use the bomb, we are only keeping it as a threat. But in reality the bomb destroys the fullness of life that Christ promised us. It destroys the life of the poor in the material sense, and it destroys the life of the rich in the spiritual sense. It crouches in us; it has possessed us. We cannot experience fullness of life as long as we live under the bomb, the most important symbol of our world and the thing our politicians fear and love, study and pay for above all things—in other words, their God.

The riches of the wealthy are not only their possessions but much more: their power of destruction. The world we live in is especially rich in death and better means of killing. The bombs stored beneath the earth and under the surface of the oceans in submarines, waiting to be used; the tons of explosives planned for every person on earth are, I believe, aimed at God. The intention behind the arms buildup is that God should finally disappear from the earth. Even the bombs that have not yet been used are directed against God. Militarism is humanity's greatest attempt to get rid of God once and for all, to unmake creation and to prevent redemption to fullness of life.

If it is true that excess things make life excessive, the way to change is to become poorer. "Sell what you have," Jesus says to the rich middle-class person, "and give it to the poor." We cannot simply fill our inner emptiness with God, as some people dream of doing through a kind of cheap spirituality. We must first be externally empty of everything that fills us to superfluity. The process of making oneself empty for God means surrendering or at least restricting all worldly possessions, money, and power. Becoming poorer and getting along with less and less power: that is repentance to life in abundance.

Jesus tried to suggest to the rich young man how to break with his own world, its attitudes and values, and with his own privileged social class. Christ poses the same question to us: How long will we continue to cooperate in the order of this world, the order of exploitation and oppression? How long will we continue to be beneficiaries and accomplices of the system governed by the "thief who comes to steal, to kill, and to spoil"? As far as my own country is concerned, this question is a little easier to answer today than it was three years ago.

I must honestly say that I would not have believed that so much liberation and life could emerge from traditional churches, which I have so often experienced as the tomb of Christ. But God raises up peacemaking sons and daughters of God even out of stones, so why not out of church congregations as well?

A few years ago many of the most thoughtful people I know longed to go to the Third World, because the struggles there were clearer, the fronts more sharply defined, the hopes more immediate. "I wish I were in Nicaragua," a student wrote me, "for a Christian life would be possible there." It seemed to many of us that we could only find Christ with the poor, and not in a First World context. But I think all this has changed somewhat. We do not live in El Salvador, but we do live under the domination of NATO. Its planning departments make decisions about our lives and those of other peoples. The false idols are presented there, and that is where our struggle must be. Our historic task is the battle for peace and against militarism. That is our share in the liberation struggles of the Third World. No one who feels allied with the poor has any reason today to despair and to plunge into senseless acts of destruction and suicide. Since the latest round of escalation of armaments, which is intended to perpetuate the rule of terror, we know where our El Salvador is . . . our Vietnam . . . our Soweto . . . our liberation struggle and our conversion from money and violence to justice and peace. Paul has another name for "fullness of life": it is all of us, "with unveiled face, reflecting the glory of the Lord" (2 Cor. 3:18). We find this glory in the faces that have turned toward justice and peace.

Many Christians believe that nonviolence is only possible in the reign of God, while war and poverty are facts of life here on earth. But those who think that way separate God from God's kingdom and wish for themselves, like the rich young man, an eternal life without justice and an abundant life without love. That is nonsense. The wealth of human persons is in their relationships with others, in being for others. The fullness of life is not diminished when we share it; instead, it multiplies itself as marvelously as did the five loaves and two fish. Christ frees us from the poverty that devours life and from the inner emptiness that sucks up vitality; he frees us for a new community in which we need not do violence to one another anymore, but can instead make one another happy. We have become one with living love and no longer need to put off eternal life to a time that is not our own.

There is a passage in Isaiah that speaks of fullness of life, its beauty and truth:

> . . . loose the bonds of wickedness,
> . . . undo the thongs of the yoke,
> . . . let the oppressed go free,
>   and . . . break every yoke.
> . . . share your bread with the hungry,
>   and bring the homeless poor into your house;
> when you see the naked, . . . cover [them],
>   and [do not] hide yourself from your own flesh.
> Then shall your light break forth like the dawn,
>   and your healing shall spring up speedily;
> your righteousness shall go before you,
>   the glory of the LORD shall be your rear guard.
>   . . .
> you shall be called the repairer of the breach,
>   the restorer of streets to dwell in. (58:6-12)

The text speaks of richness of life. Don't keep yourself in reserve, it says. Your abundance grows with your extravagance. What this text talks about is the wealth that we have in being human beings, not the wealth of possession. Wealth that consists of having things secures itself by ownership, status, and privilege. It is a wealth that has been amassed by making others poor. The rich person Isaiah describes, who shares bread with the hungry and converses with the depressed, is not rich in possessions, but in human relationships. She has many friends. The sense is not that of inner riches that enable one simply to overlook external unfreedom and poverty. The rich person, as Isaiah sees it, is fully aware of society's injustice, oppression, and destructiveness of life. But she does not accept it. Her life has direction, a clear tendency, and its direction is that all shall receive a name. In this sense a little country like Nicaragua is rich, because there abundance has arisen out of scarcity. Wealth is acquired in winning brothers and sisters for oneself.

Isaiah is not speaking of people under orders, people carrying out assignments. He is thinking of the strong, rich person who has so often been calumniated and denigrated in Christian tradition. But the prophet counts on people like that, and invites them to the beauty of a genuine, fulfilled life.

The gospel—for this text is pure gospel—is lovely. It promises a life free from despising others or oneself. A life without cynicism, a life without fear, a rich life in which every hour counts. "Then shall your light break forth like the dawn." Where you are wounded, the skin will quickly close. Even in the banality of everyday life, in the waterless desert of fossilized relationships, your soul will be satisfied and nothing will be meaningless. "Your gloom [shall] be as the noonday."

When I hear this text I am not faced with new demands, for those are old and well known. Instead, I am enticed toward fullness of life. That is the way to live; that is how I want to be. That is how I want people to think of me. I want to win such a name. When I hear the text, I remember we are strong, we can do something, we are not expendable. We need not sing, the whole year long, that we are powerless to do anything and that we are lost. We have a new song: "Then shall your light rise in the darkness, . . . you shall be like a watered garden, like a spring of water, whose waters fail not." So it should be; so it will be. I will have a name, I will receive an answer, I will no longer be a helpless, fearful thing. Instead, the world's Truth, the meaning of life, will be open for all to see. "See, here I am," God says in this text; not far away, not at some time in the future or for more fortunate people in the past, but *here* is the meaning of everything: Do not withdraw from your brothers and sisters, and then your light shall break forth like the dawn.

Christianity has nothing to say that cannot be heard in other parts of the world. "If you will remove oppression from your midst . . ." But at the same time it adds a final promise: Nothing is meaningless.

Teresa of Avila said, "All the way to heaven is heaven." At no stage of the journey, no matter how great the darkness, are you alone. If you surrender yourself to the movement of love, your strength will be multiplied. Your wealth increases the more you share it. Wherever you surrender yourself to the power of love, love is with you: life to the full.

Note

1. H. D. Thoreau, "Civil Disobedience," in *Great Short Works of Henry David Thoreau,* ed. with an introduction by Wendell Glick (New York, San Francisco and London: Harper & Row, 1982), 146.

Christianity and Post-Marxism

I. On "Post-ism"

Admittedly, the concept of post-Marxism doesn't really knock me off my feet, any more than do other ideas built on "post-ism." The labels "post-modern" and "post-Christian" do nothing to enlighten or clarify. To be "after" someone or something doesn't amount to any particular qualification. My suspicion of these post-intellectuals is that they are in the business of doing away with the question of truth and neutralizing the claims to truth contained, for example, in Christianity, Marxism, or feminism. What is the sense of emphasizing that I live after my grandmother? Is the chronological factor supposed to replace every substantial discussion—so that someone can then overtrump with the terrific discovery that she or he is a "post-post-Marxist"?

What are all these post-Marxists, post-moderns, post-Christians trying to tell us? I detect a variety of different statements. Some are saying: We had it, we know it, we don't need it anymore. *Chronos* swallows *kairos*—that different kind of historical thinking—and in this sense the post-thinkers are on their knees, if not totally prostrate in the dust, before the latest trends. I find it especially embarrassing, in respect to Marxism, when "pre-"Marxists or those I understand to be "post-"Marxists start holding forth. I want to ask them: Have you ever tried it?

Another voice from the chorus of post-theoreticians sounds like this: We had it, we loved it, we still need it, but it didn't work; we have to rethink and reshape it. I feel more closely attuned to this reforming attitude—but why shouldn't we stick with good old-fashioned Marxism? Reform is a part of every living structure of thought. Even Martin Luther, despite everything, was not a post-Christian. I sense a species of intellectual weakness when something new is not given a new name—presuming, of course, that the post-theoreticians want something new. If post-Christians want a new thing, within religion or outside of it, they ought to say so and thus identify themselves with it—presumably as non-Christians.

But are they, perhaps, standing on the doorstep of an old house, ready to leave it, yet still tied to its values, its traditions, its claims to truth? Most of the people I know, myself included, fall into this category, and this is precisely the problem we share with our Marxist friends. Our challenge arises out of a rejection of institutional rules and regulations. In the face of the Christian church and its role in the First World, I feel alienation, aversion, disgust, and sometimes even shame. I see this empirical church as a structure "from above," based on injustice and continually betraying its own truth. I often think that the church is like Judas, who handed Christ over to the established religious authorities. Sometimes I think that the church is like the other disciples who, discouraged and defeated, left Jesus alone and fled. And then there are times when I think the church is like Peter, who denied that he had ever known anything about peace and justice. Very seldom do I see the church, like Peter, shedding bitter tears.

Nevertheless, I have never regarded myself as post-Christian. I have also experienced something other than what I have just described. I have seen the church in a group of women who did not flee, who stayed, and on Easter Sunday went to the tomb because the one who had gone was not dead for them. However, my overwhelmingly bad experiences have changed my image of the church. It is not a house for me any longer; instead, it is a tent for the wandering people of God. The tent is not always where I am, but sooner or later I encounter the tent people again—on the street or in the courtroom. The sacred is not so much a building or an institution as an event, something that happens. Not long ago Daniel Berrigan, in conversation, employed the image of an umbrella that shelters us from the cold rain. Sometimes it opens too slowly, and we are left standing in the rain. Sometimes it is not very effective. Still, it is there, and I would not want to be without it. But the image of the church that continues to impress me most is that of an old woman looking for food in a garbage can—an unmarried mother with bent back, unattractive, unhealthy, of indeterminate age—my older sister, whom I need and who needs me.

I suspect that the post-Christians do not want to have anything to do with the dialectic of a religious institution. But it is just this self-contradictory experience of the *church as traitor* and the *church as sister* that stares me in the face, and I have to live with it. Post-Christianity seems to me like a slick formula that covers up the two-sided encounter with the church and reduces it to the "church from above." Then the church from below is forgotten, and with it what tradition has identified as the "mystical body of Christ."

How far can these considerations aid us in understanding Marxism as well? Is it useful for us to pay attention to the struggles between Marxist-hierarchical orthodoxy and its mystical heresies? If so, we can safely drop the notion of post-Marxism and admit instead that we still live and think, in many respects, in a pre-Marxist community of citizens, in a community divided by class, race, and sex. We are sunk deeply in the economic and spiritual apartheid that characterizes our whole life. We urgently need any kind of tool that can help us to escape.

II. What Christians Have Learned from Marxism
When asked if I'm a marxist

> I reach for the receiver every day
> dial and talk
> how different my life would be
> if the telephone had not yet been invented
> how much harder living here
> for the woman from Greece
> when she goes to the train station on Sunday.
>
> You didn't ask me
> if I'm a Bellist
> out of respect for Alexander G. Bell
> without whom we would be worse off
> even worse off I imagine
> I don't name myself after him
>
> Nor after the great inventor
> from Trier[1]

I am often impatient when believers ask me: "Are you a Marxist?" The best reply I can think of is a counter-question: "Do you brush your teeth? I mean, since the toothbrush has been invented?" How can anyone read Amos and Isaiah, and not Marx and Engels? That would be absolute ingratitude toward a God who sends us prophets with the message that to know YHWH means to do justice. Are we not obliged to use every analytic tool that can help us to comprehend injustice and at the same time reveal the victims of injustice as the possible forces for change that can break the spell of oppression for both the oppressors and the oppressed? Can we afford to ignore Marx at a time when it ought to be clear to every attentive observer of the misery in the Third World that capitalism neither can nor will satisfy hunger? Our economic system works for the rich, not for the other two-thirds of the human family. Should we, who stand in the tradition of religion and its anthropological assumptions about human dignity, not at least seek a historical alternative?

The need for a fundamental analysis comes from biblical faith in the God of justice. A theological education that awakens no sense of need for an economic theory betrays its own goal. More and more Christians are coming to understand this. They have entered into a process of taking account of Marxism and have learned simultaneously to understand their own tradition anew. At last, they have opened themselves to one of the greatest spiritual challenges to their faith and have ceased to regard that challenge as an enemy invasion in a peaceful, harmonious land. In short, after nearly a century of hate, fear, self-deception, denial, and lies, they have entered into a dialogue.

We ought not to forget that this dialogue began, not in conference halls, but in Fascist prison cells and concentration camps where Christians and Marxists met and shared suffering and hope, cigarettes and news. The dialogue among intellectuals is a latecomer, at least in Europe, where it began first in the early sixties. A Marxist-Christian dialogue has also begun, under quite different conditions, in the Third World. One precondition for this dialogue is the historical experience that neither religion nor socialism can be repressed by pure force. In the countries of Eastern Europe, religion not only survived but increased in importance, and socialism could be killed neither by Fascist concentration camps nor by CIA intrigues. But the dialogue was and is more than simply living side by side; it implies growing together and learning from one another.

In this process of encounter, Christians not only became acquainted with socioeconomic analysis, but their theology itself underwent a process of transformation. We—and this "we" includes a growing number of thoughtful Christians from the conservative camp—began at last to understand our own contribution to the various forms of oppression. There followed a massive self-criticism that often took the paralyzing form of guilt feelings. In other groups, the learning process led to a feeling of shame, which, according to Marx, is a revolutionary sentiment. Christians, especially in the Third World, joined liberation movements or at least took part in groups that fought against brutal violations of human rights. Roger Garaudy characterized the Christian-Marxist encounter in the sixties as a movement "from anathema to dialogue."[2] In the seventies, this process then moved on "from dialogue to alliance," and for many of us it is now proceeding much farther: a new Christian Socialist identity is arising in the most varied places.

In the course of this process, Christians on the one hand developed an increasingly critical attitude toward their own institutions and traditions, while on the other hand they put down deeper roots in their traditions of liberation. We have learned to use our tradition. If we do not, it will use us. This process was a genuine dialogue; that is, it was free from domination and aimed at mutual giving and receiving.

When I think back on what we have learned, theoretically and practically, I would say that, theologically speaking, we have come to understand the meaning of the incarnation in a new way. The encounter with Marxism has deepened my Christian understanding of the historical and social dimensions of human existence. As we all know, the Christian God all too often remains a disembodied heavenly being distant from history's victories and defeats, experienced only by individuals for their own happiness. This is an idealistic God who has neither a bodily nor a social dimension. This God has nothing to do with what happens to the body or to social structures. Through confrontation with philosophical materialism Christians learned to take material existence more seriously, in the twofold sense of body and society. In this way, hunger and unemployment, the military-industrial complex and its consequences for daily life strode to the forefront of theological discourse. God's becoming human can no longer be understood as a once-for-all and completed event; instead, it is a continuing process of divine self-realization in history. Marxism's critique of Christianity as an idealistic and superficial understanding of human history could now be answered anew on the basis of a new understanding of the Word made flesh: flesh understood both as body and as society. Marxists helped Christians to a better understanding of the profound being-in-the-world of Christian faith of which Bonhoeffer spoke.

What meaning does this concept have for Christians who live under socialist governments? Christians in East Germany, Poland, and Czechoslovakia have had a new opportunity to live their faith without social reward or privilege—in contrast to the capitalist countries. They experienced the end of the Constantinian era in their own lives. Their privileges were withdrawn, their schools closed, their buildings no longer maintained by the state; their tax reductions were abolished along with their tax-free, service-free income. Perhaps most painful was the fact that the society no longer accorded special respect to clergy. The dirty fist of a miner was more highly regarded than the lily-white hand of a bishop offering a blessing. Christians are now only one group among many others in society.

The dialogue encouraged Christians in Eastern Europe to see the historical shift in their lives since 1945 in theological perspective and not in an uncritical, secular manner that only considered the loss of power. Christians began to understand what had happened to them, as they left Herod's palace, where they had disported themselves for two thousand years, and returned to the stable and the manger. They did not complain about their new situation and did not denounce it as "persecution"—in contrast to Radio Free Europe and other CIA-supported institutions. Instead, they learned in a painful process to understand the situation and to accept it. Theologically, they learned to distinguish between Christian faith and ecclesial privilege, between stable and palace—between a rich and powerful church on the one side, paid by the society to legitimize oppression, militarism, exploitation, and discrimination; and a small, poor, and often underprivileged church on the other side, one that only in this way has a chance to be Christian.

From this perspective and out of this dialogue, Christians also gained a new understanding of the history of their church. Marxists like Friedrich Engels and Rosa Luxemburg had developed much clearer criteria than most church historians with which to distinguish between the Constantinian and the apocalyptic traditions in Christianity. Church history follows an internal dialectic: On the one hand there is the Constantinian tradition with its emphasis on sin as the most important faith-content of a tradition that justifies state and dominion as the will of God, since the people are not capable of freedom and self-government. On the other hand there is the apocalyptic tradition, which always springs up where the masses become aware of their power; in this tradition the emphasis is on redemption, victory over sin through the Son of Man. The Constantinian tradition sanctioned all forms of class domination, from slavery to wage-work, and it accorded the loyal church its place at the side of the current rulers. The apocalyptic tradition, however, was at the center of the revolt of a Jan Hus, as it is now the heart and soul of the Christian Socialist movement in Latin America.

This dialogue between Christians and Marxists came to a sudden end in 1968 as the Soviets marched into Prague and suppressed what Dubček had called "socialism with a human face," as dreamed of by him and many participants in the dialogue. The historic attempt to reconcile Marxism and democracy was crushed by one of the imperialist superpowers, as it was later in Chile by the efforts of the other superpower. At the same time the most open and progressive positions of Vatican Council II were watered down and retracted. The Catholic reform movement in the Netherlands was suppressed, rebellious priests transferred, the publication of radical writings by Catholic presses was stopped. John XXIII was succeeded by Paul VI. The time of hope seemed to be past; everything stagnated.

But in the meantime other forms of cooperation between Christians and Marxists had developed. They originated less with intellectuals, professors, pastors, or journalists and more with people who had organized in resistance groups focusing on the central political and social problems of the Western world and the countries dominated by it: the spreading decline of living conditions in capitalist societies, inflation, unemployment, and ecological catastrophe as well as the Vietnam war and its public or hidden military and financial support. Perhaps most important was the growing resistance to economic exploitation of the countries of the Third World. Again in the seventies, Marxists and Christians found themselves more and more frequently allied in various forms of struggle.

This struggle is like a spiral of violence. The first and most prominent form of violence is the withholding of a truly human life from the majority who are cut off from work, housing, food, health, and education. The second form of violence is the counterviolence of the oppressed. It leads to the third form of violence on the part of the state and the police, with consequent suppression and dismantling of the democratic rights for which the people had struggled so long. This third form is today characteristic of a growing number of Latin American countries: a process of creeping fascism that begins with the cutting off of democratic rights like freedom of opinion, speech, press, assembly, and organization and ends in open terror and torture.

Unfortunately, Christians seldom enter the process in the phase of counterviolence on the part of the oppressed, although there are some who work side by side with their Marxist comrades in strike committees and production cooperatives. In general, Christians first become involved when they become aware of the publicly growing fascism in their own countries, in the third phase of violence. One example was the peace committee in Chile between 1972 and 1975, the year of its banning and dissolution. Most of the members were Christians, led by Cardinal Silva and Bishop Frenz, who were active on behalf of political prisoners and so-called missing persons. The bitter truth is that it is fascism that first creates an alliance between Christians and Marxists, and not the milder forms of capitalism, although they are just as deadly in their intent. At any rate, new alliances were formed, and the cooperative work was made easier by the previous dialogue and its insight into the common struggle. Today the uncommitted, purely academic dialogue has been surpassed, and the locus of encounter and of growing community between Christians and Marxists is more likely to be the street, the big-city slum, or the prison cell than the lecture hall.

The people who enroll in this school for struggle draw on both the Christian and the Marxist traditions. It is more and more difficult and useless for them (and not only for them) to pry apart and separate their various motivations and aims into "Christian" or "Socialist." In many groups this process has already developed further than the inherited language and symbolic words may indicate. Recently a radio reporter from Arizona asked me whether I support the Sanctuary movement out of religious or political motives. I countered by asking him whether he had ever read the Bible. If so, how could he ask such a question? Did he think Jesus was a political or a religious refugee when he fled to Egypt to escape Herod's death squads? The more I read the Bible, the less I comprehend such questions.

This new consciousness and identity were especially apparent in the Nicaraguan revolution. In the struggle to overthrow the dictator, Christians there played an enormously important role. And not only that: their participation in power and responsibility for the construction of a new society were unique. The three priests who had ministerial posts in the Sandinista government were only the most obvious evidence of this. Active Catholics work in the media and in basic organizations throughout the country for a more just society. Tomas Borge, minister of the interior in Managua, expressed this new spirit, which goes beyond mere dialogue and strategic alliance, especially clearly: "The revolution is confronting the theology of death."[3] He knew very well that capitalism is served not only by death squads, the mining of harbors, or napalm bombs, but also by an obliging theology that neutralizes victims, silences hunger and oppression, and individualizes hope. For those who have chosen sides in this fight and who have committed themselves to the liberating power of God in history, such a pre-Marxist understanding of theology is in no sense neutral—it is a *theologia de la muerte!*

III. Marxists Listening to Christians: What Things Will Be Fulfilled

All those who have taken part in the process of dialogue I have just described know that Christians hesitated a long time before criticizing their Marxist comrades. In fact, they denied that they could teach the Marxists anything. The general attitude was: We, as bourgeois, as Christians, as religious socialists, have no right to speak out or to introduce our own tradition. I think, though, that we have now changed our attitude. Perhaps it is because in the meantime we are catching up with our responsibilities and thus have earned the moral right to speak as revolutionaries. In a long and painful process we have learned both to free ourselves from our tradition and to make it our own. Now it is time not only to make our contribution to what already exists, but also, in the sense of the revolutionary process, to make suggestions for its improvement.

Two examples drawn from present struggles make this claim concrete. The first is again related to the liberation movements in Latin America. The blood of the martyrs is a stronger witness than words could ever be to the reality of historical struggles. The son of Felipe and Mary Barreda, two leaders of the local church in Esteli, Nicaragua, said after his parents were murdered by the Contras: "They became revolutionaries in order to be Christians. Thanks to their example I know that I cannot be a real revolutionary unless I am a Christian, and that I will not really be a Christian unless I am a revolutionary."[4]

My own experiences in the European peace movement also testify to decisive changes in the relationship between the secular Left, with its traditional antireligious orientation, and the religious Left, which is becoming more and more visible. It is a simple fact that the peace movement originated neither in the labor unions nor in student organizations, but often—at least in West Germany and the Netherlands—in part of the Lutheran church. I sense that practicing Christians are much more respected at present than they were even five years ago. The "cultured despisers" have, just recently, learned to distinguish between the theologies of liberation—also a seed-bed of a theology of peace—and Christian fascist tendencies as represented by the Moral Majority in the United States. My own reflections on the changing positions within Marxism grew out of these struggles for peace and justice. Here I will characterize the changes within Marxism that may (or may not) be due to the participation of Christians in these struggles, but that in any event make the process of our growing together much easier.

One of the most acute problems for all who are well acquainted with Marxism is the search for those who are prepared to remake society. I will confine myself here to the First World. Who is the revolutionary subject today, in a time when industrial workers no longer have only their chains to lose? André Gorz addressed this question in his "Farewell to the Proletariat." This adieu to the revolutionary power of the nineteenth-century labor movement contains a critique of orthodox Marxism and its class analysis. The new social movements, whether feminist, ecological, or pacifist, whether originating from the economically, racially, or sexually oppressed, cut across class lines. The central issues of the struggle have also shifted from assembly line and factory to the fight for survival outside the employment structure. The problems now are, for example, health, child care, education, sexuality, housing, transportation, rent control and subsidies, consumer rights, and many more. The leaders of these struggles are no longer only the white male adults in the cities.

This shift in emphases and leadership has also reached the orthodox Marxist parties and moved them toward Eurocommunism, which differs from the old communist parties essentially on two points: first, the acceptance of the system of parliamentary elections as a means to a "peaceful way to socialism," in contrast to the necessity for armed revolution; second, the abandonment of the "dictatorship of the proletariat," which hitherto had been a tenet not subject to discussion. These democratic openings require a decentralization of power. And this tendency opens Marxist thinking to those who do not intend to surrender democratic control over the power of the state, but instead wish to extend it into the economic sphere.

Further changes are in process, affecting not only party lines but political culture in general. Perhaps the most important shift in post-Stalinist Marxism is the new evaluation of culture. In present Marxist thought we can see a revival of Gramsci's work; in particular his concept of the "organic intellectual," a contrast to the avant-garde leader, is attracting Marxists of different orientations. There is a new emphasis on the cultural means to revolutionary thought. Art, music, and philosophy as self-expression of the people now play a different role than in classical Marxism with its notorious tendency to economic reductionism.

In connection with this shift toward culture, the attitude toward religion has changed and will continue to change. If local reporters, social workers, or nutrition experts play a new role in the movement today, why not the local priest or pastor? Religion is a notable factor in popular culture. Why should it not serve also as a vehicle of revolutionary thought? Only nonorganic intellectuals or theoreticians feel themselves superior to religion; only these white, male, city-bred, culturally bourgeois, educated, abstract beings regard religion as something inferior and connect it with the sex and color of the powerless, or generally with unenlightened phases of human history. Any self-critical understanding of Marxism, on the contrary, must today admit that atheism has affinities to a certain class that overvalues reason, achievement, productivity, and progress.

If Marxists now turn away from their traditional position in this regard, this is not to be considered some kind of tactical maneuver designed to win over a couple of useful idiots from the Christian side. I see it instead as a gradual recognition of the reality of immanent transcendence in human life. Marxists are coming, more and more, to appreciate the accession of strength drawn from the source of life, which we traditionally call God. What our priests and missionaries failed to accomplish—namely, the conversion of socialists to a God who is "fullness of life" for all—could still be possible for the comrades who suffer and struggle alongside one another. Maybe Christians have the chance, for the first time in the historical struggle of the dispossessed, to make God more visible, especially for those who are ready to give their lives for the least of their sisters and brothers.

Thoughtful Marxists are asking themselves today whether the historical union between Marxism and atheism is still necessary; whether the demand to give up God, religion, and everything sacred does not play directly into the hands of those who want to maintain the status quo. Many people in both East and West share the conviction that religion and socialism are incompatible. But the political culture of their subjects is as different from these ideological propositions as is the religious culture of greater hope and deeper love. In the seventies, Fidel Castro proclaimed that the revolution would not take place against or without the Christians, but only with them. At the end of the seventies, the revolution reached Nicaragua. What has happened there in the meantime is irreversible.[5] The spirit that has seized the people of Nicaragua is much greater than the "enlightened self-interest" of a Marxist ethician. They are ready to die for the revolution. I sense that the rational language of theory cannot quite grasp the spark of this spirit by which they live and—when necessary—die. If we are really to understand what is happening there and in so many other places, we need a different language. Even hard-boiled Marxists feel some of the effect of these sparks.

Perhaps a day will come when the theology of death rules and exploits, militarizes and subdues the whole world with its threat of the first strike. Then people will honor Death as the true ruler and bow down to it, not only in the Pentagon, but even in New Zealand, El Salvador, the Netherlands, and everywhere. In that day of absolute destruction, Marxism will need more than a rational theory. We all need, at a particular point in our individual, national, and world history, something beyond the crucifixion. I do not say this in a triumphalist spirit, but with fear and trembling. I wish that my Marxist friends could share my belief in the resurrection of the dead, so that they could go on fighting and suffering under the shadow of the crosses that stand all around us.

When the names of the martyrs are remembered in church or in public assemblies, the people in Latin America respond after each name: *"presente."* "Oscar Romero?" *"Presente."* "Ita Ford?" *"Presente."* It is a powerful symbol of this new identity. It is an affirmation of the resurrection—with no Platonist superstructure. It is an invitation of the Christian community to its Marxist sisters and brothers, a challenge to them to overcome their intellectual atheism and to affirm the God of life. The time for this liturgy has arrived. "Karl Marx?" *"Presente!"*

Notes

1. From D. Sölle, *fliegen lernen: Poems* (West Berlin: Fietkau, 1979).

2. Roger Garaudy, *From Anathema to Dialogue: A Marxist Challenge to the Christian Churches,* trans. Luke O'Neill (New York: Herder & Herder, 1966). Orig. ed. De l'anathéme au dialog (Paris: Plon, 1965).

3. Tomas Borge, "The Revolution Confronts the Theology of Death," *Christianity and Revolution: Tomás Borge's Theology of Life,* trans. Andrew Reding (Maryknoll, N.Y.: Orbis, 1987), 96–107.

4. "Eine Heiligenlegende: Felipe und Mary Barreda," in D. Sölle and L. Schottroff, *Die Erde gehört Gott: Texte zur Bibelarbeit von Frauen* (Reinbek bei Hamburg: Rowohlt, 1985), 92–99.

5. This article, written before the historic changes in Eastern Europe in 1989, may explain the spiritual presuppositions behind them.

The Rose Has
No Why

A MYSTICAL APPROACH TO
THE QUESTION OF LIFE'S MEANING

I would like to begin this essay with some personal notes, and I do not in the least apologize for doing so. I consider the separation of the personal from the professional, of one's own experience from reflections that then vaunt themselves as "scientific" philosophical-theological thought, to be a fatal male invention, the overcoming of which is a task for any serious theology that intends to be a theology of both women and men.

In August 1984 some friends and I visited Milan Machoveć at his vacation home. We did not know him. In the days before this meeting I had thought about his book *On the Meaning of Human Life,*[1] in which he gave a description and critique of the most important historical definitions of meaning: the religious, the Epicurean, the Stoic, the utopian-optimistic, and the resignative descriptions of life, with commentary on those who advance these positions at the present time. In a second part, called "Perspectives," he then attempted to formulate a definition of meaning within particular areas of living where the sense of significance is threatened and where life appears to become meaningless: in the cosmos, in alienated labor, in socialist systems threatened by the cult of personality.

I recalled a certain ambivalence that I had thought I detected in the book, between a "meta-religious" framing of the question and a type of religiosity I sensed in this pioneer thinker of the Christian-Marxist dialogue. What would he say today? What does it do to one's sense of the significance of one's own life if one is forbidden to work, is censored, spied upon, and kept under surveillance? Is there anything, to use Machoveć's own words, that can take the place of obsolete religious faith without causing the person to be "impoverished and fall below the historical level of religion?"[2] Is there a substitute for religion that hangs on and reformulates its values without retaining its illusory character? Like many Christian Marxists, Machoveć sought "not merely a synthesis of rational science and philosophy," but "something that penetrates the whole of life *integrally* and *intensively* in the same way as does religion, gives it unity and lends people a certain inner power and strength with which to bear life's hardships and the blows of fate." It was a question "of a new, non-religious conception of the whole person, of a new unity between reason, emotion and will."[3]

I really wanted to ask Machoveć whether he could formulate the meaning of life today in exactly the same way as he had then, on the verge of the Prague Spring and long before the onset of winter in 1968. But I never got to ask the question. There was no pause in which to introduce it. What was bubbling and boiling in him, as he posed questions and answered them himself, was much more forceful than my perhaps rather pedantic question. The truth is that in the course of the conversation I forgot my question. The rose has no why.

When I later tried to figure out what Machoveć had to say now, twenty years after his book, on the subject of the meaning of human life, I could not get beyond the ambiguity I have already mentioned, which I will formulate as follows: Machoveć, as a "post-religious" Marxist thinker, postulates that we can only *give* a meaning to life; the concept's impulse is precisely to sustain this meaning-bestowing, meaning-creating act against the resistance of the powers of death and destruction that are everywhere on the march. But this is contradicted by the fact that he seems at the same time—and even anteriorly, in the ontological sense—to *accept* the meaning of life. He is borne by the power of life, at home in a historically developed European humanism that by no means needed to create and produce everything. Do we give meaning to life, or is the meaning already there? I want to answer this question with the aid of Goethe and

Angelus Silesius, because I think that the panentheistic-mystical position has the widest possibilities of any religion in the post-modern period.

If I were to summarize my feelings about Milan Machoveć in one word, I would say that he is "devout." What does the word mean here? I prefer the English word *devout* to the synonym *pious,* in order to emphasize the element of self-surrender, of engagement, of devotion to life. Goethe used the word *Weltfrömmigkeit* (devotion to the world); he spoke of the "sense of God's omnipresence," of God's being everywhere, in phenomena of nature, in the relationship between human persons. The experience of God as present in this life is a way of describing the meaning of life that is opposed to the modern, rationalistic way of thinking whereby it is we who create life's meaning.

Pantheism and Goethe's nature mysticism, influenced by Spinoza, are bound up with the question of meaning, and thus also of human creative energies, the human capacity to bestow meaning, conceived pantheistically as gift, as grace, as sharing in the origins of life. Goethe, who preferred to avoid the word *grace,* said in a conversation with Eckermann: "All productivity of the highest kind, every important Aperçu, every invention, every great fruitful and consequential thought, is subject to no individual's power and is superior to all earthly might.—The human being must regard such things as unhoped-for gifts from above, as pure children of God, which he is to receive with joyful gratitude and to revere.—It is related to the demonic, which dominates and treats him as it pleases, and to which he unconsciously surrenders when he thinks he is acting on his own impulse."[4]

Life is not something that simply is; it is given, and the highest form of living, which Goethe understands as productivity, is also a gift that, in principle, is not always at our disposal. This seems to me to be important, because religion and devotion are articulated here. Goethe transferred the treasures that have expressed themselves in the Christian religion into his pantheistic religion of humanity. This procedure of saving the treasures of religion by transferring them is also what Machoveć is doing philosophically. He witnesses to a knowledge that life is not made, but given to us. Goethe calls this gratitude and reverence. The fundamental experience is that it is not I who create my life, and therefore I cannot take yours away from you either. Nor can I arbitrarily decide when elderly people are old enough to be given a lethal injection. There is a kind of reverence that preserves this point: that human dignity is not created by us, but exists before us. It is not derivable from anything else and does not depend on someone else's agreement—the state's, let us say.

People are always in search of language for such experiences as those of reverence, devotion, or what Goethe calls the "need to give homage," and the historic religions have offered formulae—otherwise they would never have been able to acquire so much influence over human beings. Obviously, they have not gained their power *only* through lies, deception, subjugation, and clerical domination, but because they had, in substance, something to say and they connected it with just these human needs, which we can summarize as "religious needs."

In a man like Goethe, one who is so free of ties to his own class, to his own nation, who is quite independent in religious questions— precisely in such a man we can clearly see how deeply religiosity was rooted and how it impelled him to this devotion to the world and nature, this Spinozism in his own terms. When Goethe speaks of the Inscrutable that is to be revered, or of the "Vengeance," as he likes to call it, I believe that mystical features are in play. He knows well enough that there is a world of language, but that beyond language something exists that we cannot utter. Goethe spoke on the border between the utterable and the unutterable, a sign of this mystical religiosity. In his conversations with Eckermann, for example, the latter tells him an ornithological story about a robin that fed two wrens that had fallen from their nest. Goethe, deeply touched, says: "If anyone hears that and is not moved, Moses and the prophets cannot help him. That is what I call the omnipresence of God, who has diffused part of his infinite love and implanted it everywhere."[5] That is an expression of faith in creation, in the goodness of creation, in the words that conclude the biblical creation story: "See, everything was very good."

Goethe's devotion to the world was nourished by this faith. Is such a faith still feasible? What would be the preconditions for an answer to the question about the meaning of life that would not only reply, in a Promethean and enlightened manner, with a definition to settle the question, but in Franciscan devotion with the acceptance of a good creation that is meaningful in itself, or, to put it in theological terms, a creation that praises God?

Angelus Silesius, in his *Cherubinic Wanderer*, shaped one type of condensed mystical response. He adopts the image of the rose, mystical symbol of the blood of Christ. In a similar couplet Johannes Scheffler expressed the symbolic content of the rose:

> The rose which here on earth is now perceived by me,
> Has blossomed thus in God from all eternity[6]

In the visual arts the symbol of the rose is related to the blood of Christ, captured in a bowl and transformed in the sacrament, or else the rose directly symbolizes Christ's wounds. The statement that the rose has bloomed "in God forever"[7] means that the Word, the Logos, Christ, was with God from all eternity (Prologue to John's Gospel). But this dogmatic interpretation is, of course, not all. The verse also speaks out of a spirituality of creation that is distinctive for the mystics. To "see" the rose—in the sense of the Johannine *idou* ("see for yourself!")—means to experience the presence of God here and now, to perceive God with external sight as love here present. A natural event, a botanical species, communicates God.

The finite is quite capable of comprehending the infinite. Nature is a book in which we can read; it is not closed or hostile. It is no neutral object to be made use of; instead, it is a mirror in which we recognize ourselves, a reflection of the Life that communicates itself.

What does the rose tell us?

> The rose hath no why; it blooms because it blooms,
> It noteth not itself, asks not if it be seen.[8]

In this couplet Angelus Silesius summarizes his answer to the question of the meaning of life. Whereas we ordinarily think we are more than a rose, belonging to a higher order of being, he makes the rose the fundamental image and exemplar of true being. It is without purpose, not there for some other reason, not for use, but meaningful in itself. "For what is beautiful appears holy in itself," as Eduard Mörike says in "On a Lamp." Being is not a means to something else; it is justified in itself. It requires no recognition from outside that would bestow value on it; the rose "asks not if it be seen." Nor has it any need of the dividedness of self-reflection in an observing subject and an observed object; it does not need to take note of itself. Wholeness and unity are essential features of this creature.

The concept of being "without a why" stems from Meister Eckhart; being *sunder warumbe* is for Eckhart a description of essential being, of the "innermost ground" in which purposes, even religious ones like eternal blessedness, have no further part to play and in which the dividedness that is characteristic of evil, which is disunited with itself, is abandoned.

In a famous passage, Eckhart wrote in clarification of the *sunder warumbe*:

> If anyone were to ask life over a thousand years, "Why are you alive?" the only reply could be: "I live so that I may live." This happens because life lives from its own foundation and rises out of itself. Therefore it lives without a reason so that it lives for itself. Whoever asked a truthful person who accomplishes deeds from his or her own foundation, "Why do you accomplish your deeds?" that person, if he or she were to reply correctly, would say only: "I accomplish so that I can accomplish." God begins where the creature comes to an end. Now God longs for nothing from you more than that you should emerge from yourself in accord with your being as a creature, and that you should admit God within yourself.[9]

I want to emphasize this last point through an experience of my own. For many years I have been engaged in the peace movement, and the question that is asked me most often in this connection is, of course, the one about success: What is the point of it all? "You won't change anything anyway!" is the form in which I most often meet Eckhart's question, "Why do you accomplish your deeds?" It has become more and more clear to me that in the face of a certain cynicism, which can be objective or even subjective, arguments in favor of certain ways of acting are simply no use. A normal, working journalist, who has nothing in his or her head beyond the questions, "What do you get for that, who pays you?" and "What will you achieve by doing that?" can have nothing more than sympathy, at best, for such a hopeless undertaking as the struggle for more justice and peace; our next defeat is certain. Any thinking that is oriented solely toward success is essentially cynical.

But the rose has no why, and one has to do some things *sunder warumbe*, even when they meet with no success now. There is an inner strength of being-at-peace that cannot make the goal orientation of action the measure of all things. All nonviolent action in a violent world participates, in this sense, in the "without a why" of the rose.

In a mysticism thus understood, then, the contradiction is eliminated between the Promethean action directed toward self-realization and the creation that realizes itself in blooming. You can see this in the faces of the young people who today are carried from the roadway, in Mutlangen or Greenham Common, are beaten, imprisoned, and condemned.[10] I remember a rose that bloomed in my country's darkest hour when I say: The white rose is blooming now.[11]

Notes

1. Milan Machoveć, *On the Meaning of Human Life* (1971).
2. Ibid., 35.
3. Ibid., 31.
4. J. W. Goethe, *Conversations with Johann P. Eckermann*, 11 March 1828.
5. Ibid., 8 October 1827.
6. Angelus Silesius, *Cherubinic Wanderer* (1675) I, 108.
7. The little word *in*, saying that the rose has bloomed eternally "in God," points toward the expression that has become current in recent discussions of mysticism, the notion of panentheism (i.e., everything is in God, but God is more than the world) as opposed to pantheism (i.e., everything is God, transcendence and immanence dissolve into one another). Most Christian mystics (especially, among German mystics, Meister Eckhart) were wrongly hereticized as pantheists; in reality they were panentheists. Cf. the pioneering book by Matthew Fox, *Breakthrough: Meister Eckhart's Creation Spirituality in New Translation* (Garden City, N.Y.: Doubleday, 1980).
8. Silesius, *Cherubinic Wanderer.*
9. Meister Eckhart, *Deutsche Predigten und Traktate,* 3d ed. (Munich, 1969), Sermon 6, 180. For the English translation, see Fox, *Breakthrough*, 201.
10. Mutlangen, Suevia, and Greenham Common, United Kingdom, are towns where atomic first strike weapons were deployed. Massive actions of protest and civil disobedience have taken place since the early 1980s.
11. The White Rose was a group of young German resisters against Hitler based in Munich, 1942–43. See Inge Scholl, *The White Rose,* trans. Arthur R. Schultz, intro. by Dorothee Sölle, 2d ed. (Middletown, Conn.: Wesleyan University Press, 1983).

We Never Promised You a Rose Garden

In Mutlangen in April 1984 they built a new mass crematorium that can destroy more than six million people in a few minutes. We, the European peace movement and our allies in the United States, are fighting against this installation for general cremation.

Not long ago we could still take walks across the heath at Mutlangen. Now the military has seized the Mutlangeners' garden. Military rights break down citizens' freedom. The occupiers have the power and they take away the citizens' gardens and recreation areas, and this is happening from Göttingen to Mutlangen. The military take the gardens from the subjugated people in order to protect their cremation tools. The occupying power and its local assistant helpers take people's sons away to teach them how to use the means of mass destruction. They take away our freedom of information, one inch at a time: German television viewers may not watch the revelatory film, "The Day After," seen by millions in the United States and in England. They have to go to the movie theaters if they want to see it. Some of what I am now publishing in book form is taken from a manuscript prepared for a German radio program that fell victim to censorship.

A majority in the national parliament in Bonn made a decision in November 1983[1] that is contrary to the national and human interests of our people. It is an appointment with national suicide, something unique in human history. Our lives are now dependent on the working of Soviet computers; if they malfunction, at worst we will experience "the day after," which we are not allowed to see on television. At best there will be no day after for us. Our human interest would be to feed the hungry and to support the peoples who are struggling for self-determination. Instead, we have bound ourselves to a politics of alliance, an alliance for economic exploitation that, whenever it does not work right, turns to terror and torture.

The dirty, undeclared war that our alliance partner is now carrying on in Nicaragua shows us what this league means: attack commandos, kidnapping, rape, electric torture of people who are no threat to anybody, have never installed any missiles, and have abolished the death penalty for their torturers. Nicaragua, a country whose most important export nowadays is hope for the poor, is being attacked, bombed, and economically destroyed by our ally.

These headline stories from the fall of 1983 are examples of what the British historian Edward P. Thompson recognized as the most important tendency of our epoch: "exterminism," the drive toward mass destruction. Are the leadership elites—who, of course, "all want peace"—pushing for the extermination of life from the face of the earth? There are very few conscious and frank cynics like Zbigniew Brzezinski, who explained that he could not occupy his position as U.S. national security advisor if he were not prepared to push the exterminating button without hesitation. Exterminism in his case is the willingness to push the button; for most others, and for the millions of people who still believe in and follow this leadership elite, it is a more unconscious drive, a kind of craze for more death for other people, which is supposed to protect and enrich their own lives. They are dependent on their drugs, like addicts. They are addicted to the bomb, they adore it, they sacrifice everything for it. At the center of our culture stands the bomb, that phallic death symbol, the expression of industrialism and of patriarchy.

Exterminism is not only a plan for the future, but the historic project of the richest and most powerful nations on earth. They are already at work on the eradication of our culture at least, but probably of all life on earth as well. I will mention the three most important facts that characterize our epoch:

1. Half of humanity is absolutely impoverished. The rich, industrialized north sees to it that 10 percent of the population is starving, while another third lives below the minimum necessary for a decent existence. Capitalism, as the economically and technologically stronger system, has proved itself incapable of solving the problem of hunger. No one today can any longer close his or her eyes to this fact.

2. Nature, the basis of our life on this planet Earth, is being increasingly destroyed day by day. We in the major cities of the West can continue to fool ourselves about this by means of a still functioning repair system, but for the poor and for the impoverished nations the ecological catastrophe is already reality. The dying forests here at home make clear what is at stake in the eradication of our fellow creatures, the plants and animals.

3. The arms race between the two superpowers, led by the West, has brought us to a situation in which the extermination of the entire population of the earth is possible at any moment. There are over forty pounds of explosives for every person on earth, and that is still not nearly enough for the exterminists: they "need" more. The extirpation of all higher life on earth is "thinkable" and is being prepared. In the past, a buildup of armaments has led in almost every case to war.

These three most important facts—the impoverishment of the majority of the world's population, the destruction of nature, and the most gigantic militarism of all time—are, at any rate, exciting a growing resistance; the potential for protest today extends far into the conservative camp. To overcome it, the exterminists need something other than a nation of free citizens, and so exterminism is more and more visibly accompanied by the elimination of democracy and the installation of the surveillance state in place of civil society. The power of giant bureaucratic structures continually intervenes in people's lives—planning, ordering, regulating. Every attempt at criticism, protest, or resistance is repressed by means of the most modern technologies.

Every man and every woman who opposes the three basic tendencies listed above, even in the most harmless form, such as a signature on a petition or participation in a legitimate and publicly registered demonstration, is putting him- or herself in danger today. About ten years ago the police and secret services in West Germany were massively enhanced. Today, video systems survey every demonstration almost uninterruptedly. Anyone who hopes to become a civil servant is one day confronted with statements about his or her previous life; mere participation in expressions of political opinion is foundation for suspicion of disloyalty to the state. A teacher is removed for allowing pacifist ideas from Kurt Tucholsky, Erich Kästner, and others to be read at a high school graduation celebration. A schoolgirl who carries a poster criticizing Franz Josef Strauss is not allowed to graduate from her college preparatory school.

In the most important media, critical voices are silenced, and after a while the scissors begin to work ahead of time in the heads of the editors, who prefer to leave out a topic or omit certain authors who could bring trouble. The mass media have taken a turn in recent years toward more entertainment, more shows, more mind-numbing little games, and although there are still parks and niches where opposition is articulated, an attempt is made through the politics of the media to prevent the three basic facts of exterminism from coming to people's attention; instead, they are to be regarded as an unavoidable fate.

Besides controlling alert and active citizens through surveillance, shaping people's perception of reality through means adapted to the media, and the manipulation of language, there is still a further central point of technological-bureaucratic power: Computer technology has so refined and perfected the ability of the state or of other powerful groups to exercise control that a close-textured, nearly solid apparatus for oppression has come into being. Secret services, informers, telephone taps and listening devices, and the electronic storage of information have not been directed at the population as a whole—as in Orwell's *1984*—but they have been turned on those who deviate from computerized normality, all those who behave in any way that could be called strange or conspicuous. Deviation includes the tiniest psychic disturbance or illness; frequent changes of address; homosexuality among men; change of partner; political or labor union activities; conspicuous talking at work; membership in Amnesty International— it would be easy to expand the list. Every form of resistance to exterminism in its three dominant forms is controllable today. There are no more mountains to which the freedom fighters can withdraw, as was the case throughout most of European history.

If we are really in the process of arming ourselves to death, starving others to death, and exploiting our earth to death, the question arises, Who is capable of resistance and of peace? I would like to point in this connection to two developments of recent years that give me hope. One is the convergence of the peace and Third World movements. More and more people are seeing the connections between Pershing II missiles in Mutlangen and starving children in El Salvador. The peace movement itself is an alliance, above party and group identities, of many people who are anything but leftists by nature and who have no precise political consciousness of neo-colonial oppression of the peoples of the Third World. But the movement politicizes these people and causes them, often within a few weeks' time, to learn the lessons that normally take years to comprehend. The situation on this point is clearer here than in the United States, where the Freeze movement had a strong middle-class character; it was a "doctor's movement" and tended to shy away from connections with other political themes.

My second observation concerns the women in the peace movement. In contrast to the situation in other groups, women have become active for the cause of peace and are no longer underrepresented in this movement. That is not always publicly evident, because sexism and the oppression of women do not suddenly drop away from the men who engage themselves for the cause of peace. It is clear that a peace activist does not naturally grow out of his acquired sexism because of his antimilitarist convictions. This process requires an increase of awareness and sensitivity. Even the friends of peace have to learn to listen to those who are not normally heard. Where, if not in the movement for more peace and democracy, could we bring in our demands—for example, that we as women might become visible? I keep meeting women who apologize for the fact that they are only now, so late, "getting involved." Their learning process is astonishing, and their radicalizing, once they have understood what is at stake, is unstoppable. They have not let themselves be discouraged by the defeat suffered by peace in the Bonn parliament on November 22, 1983. They will go on with their protest, with their incitement to "demoralization of the military forces," to borrow an expression from the Nazis.

At a writers' meeting in Heilbronn in December 1983, I had an experience that nourishes this hopeful perspective. I had been through a spooky scene: we had tried to hand a letter to Colonel Brown, the camp commander of the American missile base there. Brown had refused our request for an informational meeting because he did not want to get involved in internal German affairs. The participants in the meeting at Heilbronn answered him as follows:

"You know our history, and you know that the U.S. Army came to this country to liberate us from Hitler's dictatorship, not to create new dependencies and new injustice. They came to our country to put an end to a Holocaust, and they certainly did not remain here in order to prepare for an atomic holocaust. But this is what you are doing when you threaten Eastern Europe from here with nuclear weapons and thereby expose us in this thickly settled region to deadly danger."

Since we could not hand over the letter, we taped it to the fence: humbly, as if we were begging a feudal lord to listen graciously to us, and conjuring up at the same time the worst memories from the past. On the one side was the camp with its many fences, its roadblocks, the orders to shoot, and on the other side were the German writers, including a seventy-eight-year-old Jewish woman, Grete Weil, whose husband died in Mauthausen, and Luise Rinser, who was arrested by the Nazis in 1944, accused of demoralizing the troops. When Dieter Lattmann spoke the words "concentration camp," Günter Grass added: "Only now those of us on the outside are the inmates."

At this meeting we tried to take some first steps toward learning how to resist. It seems to me that the suggestion first made by Grass and adopted by all of us, that we call for refusal of military service, is important because it does not arise out of a radical pacifist attitude, but from a consistent nuclear pacifism. As long as the German army, in defiance of the constitution, which forbids an offensive war, keeps weapons ready that are purely offensive in nature, and trains soldiers in the use of those weapons, it is the obligation of democrats to give more obedience to the constitution than to the plans of the Pentagon. A retired general of the German army, General Vollmer, explained for us writers not only the technical capabilities of the Pershing II missiles, but also their strategic applications in the offensive war that, since the development of the new "Airland Battle 2000" strategy, has replaced the old flexible response. If the German army were to abandon atomic and chemical weapons and return to its original duty of defense, then according to this idea there would no longer be any reason to refuse military service.

At a rally on November 21, 1983, the first day of the parliamentary debate about the stationing of the missiles, I tried to express what causes me to hope for these great steps. It is a text that has grown out of the new culture of peace and of women:

"We never promised you a rose garden, dear friends. When we began, after that dark day in the history of Europe, December 12, 1979,[2] to seek a different peace from the one that is founded on crimes against the poor, enmity against the neighbor, destruction of the environment, and the readiness to commit collective suicide, we knew that we could not smile away in an instant, like flower children, the hostile images and the anxieties about security that beset our political opponents in this country. We also knew that the greater political foe, the power of militarism that now controls the United States, would not abjure world domination by means of bombs and gas for our sakes. We knew, in fact, that we were starting on a long road that demands sacrifice, restrictions, isolation, making ourselves look silly, criminalization and exclusion from our jobs and professions. It took a certain amount of faith to think that nonviolence is stronger than all the weapons that can be invented, and that love has more power than the greatest military might of all times.

"How will we deal with this defeat? There is a prayer from Nicaragua that goes: 'Lead us not into the temptation to sadness, routine, and hate.' Everyone who works in the peace movement knows the temptations to despair, to function at a minimum level, or to petrify into cold hate. How much worse must this temptation be in a country that today, only a few years after its liberation, is threatened by the terror of that military power that gently colonizes us. Liberated Nicaragua is a symbol for us all of the peace that is built not on militarism, but on justice. How much longer? We are afraid that the United States, as in Grenada, will again trample on the treaties of international law and the democratic rules of the American constitution and will bring about another bloodbath. The stationing of the missiles here and the intervention in Central America are two sides of the same great-power politics, and our resistance against the compulsory nuclearizing of Europe is also resistance to the rape of the countries of the Third World that have tried to free themselves. The bombs here in the First World and the consequences in the Third World are the expression of one and the same system of violence and terror. Whoever stations missiles also permits torture in the name of national security.

"How will we deal with this defeat in our parliament? In a word: It makes us stronger. We will continue to grow. More and more people from the conservative side are listening to us and letting their own consciences speak. More and more members of the German army see that they are not serving the national interest of our people by submitting to a military strategy of limited nuclear war. More and more people in labor unions understand that the time has come to strike and to sabotage the arms buildup. Every human being has a conscience and reason. Anyone can shut off and not use one or both of these gifts for a time, but over the long term it is impossible. The parliamentary representatives who today have voted for the arms buildup must know that by doing so they are advancing the militarization of the whole world that has been planned by the United States government. I ask myself how these people can look their own children in the face today. They can't even protect a single tree if they surrender our country step by step to the occupying power for its war games.

They surely can have no relationship to the truth if they have to ignore every offer from the other side, or twist it into falsehood, in order to follow orders from the United States, with no regard for the numbers of Soviet SS-20s.

"The defeat we have suffered in the parliament is a defeat for the country. The opinion of the majority of the population has not been respected. Our answer is resistance. As long as the vital interests of the population are ignored by the government, we will carry out civil disobedience and make the organs of state accustomed to nonviolence—something quite unfamiliar to them as well as to the people who have been fettered far too long by resignation and the fear of superiors, who share our opinion but still cling to the godless 'but there is nothing anyone can do.' We have no reason for resignation. None of us should burn ourselves, neither with gasoline nor with despair. The struggle will go on! We will hinder, stall, and finally reverse the stationing of the means of mass destruction (Greenham Common). In monthly days of resistance, we will blockade the military installations of this country. We will refuse to cooperate with state offices, we will refuse taxes and military service, medical catastrophe preparations, and education for hatred of the enemy, we will hold silent vigils for peace, and in contrast to the gentlemen in the Pentagon, we will know what we are praying for.

"The gentle water breaks the stone. God is not the stone whom people treat as if they were still in the Stone Age; the peace movement does not believe in this God of stones, weapons, and violence anymore. There is a conversion from the way of violence. God is the water, without which there can be no life. Therefore we will win one day, even in this land that believes in violence. The gentle water breaks the stone."

Notes

1. The decision was to accept the stationing of Pershing and Cruise missiles in Germany. The final vote was taken on December 12.

2. See note 1 above.

The White Rose
Is Blooming

Honorable Judge, Mr. District Attorney, Dear Friends of Peace!
On Hiroshima Day, August 6 of last year, we—about fifteen people—
sat down in front of the military installation in Mutlangen where
today new and bigger Hiroshimas are being prepared. For a few hours
we impeded the preparations for the crime and the training of participants. That is why I stand before this court today. My intention
has been called "reprehensible," my nonviolent sitting has been, by
means of a manipulation of language that is unique even in German
history, which is not entirely bereft of such twists, termed "violence."

The court appears as the extended arm of state power, which, to
employ a theological expression, serves the "project of death": it
carries out the preparations for war with precision and brutality. More
bombs, more poison gas, more research for SDI [Strategic Defense
Initiative] on the one side, and more social destruction and starvation
in the poor countries on the other side—that is the great project of
death that is to be legally justified and protected here in the district
court at Schwäbisch Gmünd. The project of death is militarism, the
cancer that is overrunning and stifling our country, whose metastases
are invading every area of life: medicine and city planning, street

layout and industrial production, education and culture, theology and law as well. Militarism—that is, the ascendancy of military thinking, the elevation of so-called security questions above every other part of life—is robbing the citizens of their recreational areas and garden plots while at the same time it cuts off young people's freedom to learn and to think. If they are lucky, they may still read Tolstoy or Tucholsky, Mahatma Gandhi or Jesus—but they may not apply the Sermon on the Mount, they are forbidden to live it.

Is the legal system really supposed to be free from this cancer? I am thinking, in the realm of international law, of the refusal of the United States even to listen to the World Court at The Hague in the case of Nicaragua, and I am thinking at the national level of our constitution, which says in Paragraph 26, Number 1: "Actions that are adapted to and deliberately performed for the purpose of disturbing the peaceful life of nations in community, especially the preparation of an offensive war, are unconstitutional. They are to be punished."

Exactly ten days ago, even before the Americans began to bomb Tripoli and Benghazi, the convoys left here again, equipped with nuclear warheads and all that goes with them, and with computer steering mechanisms. They are standing ready to fire, as a support to the bombing of the civilian population in Libya. That is a clear signal to the Soviet Union: should they attempt to support Libya, the first strike against them would come from German soil. And the court sees itself obliged to protect these weapons and the policy behind them. It does not bring accusations against those who disturb the peaceful life of nations in community, or those who do not fulfill their obligation to avert damage from the German people. Instead, they accuse and criminalize the conscientious minority, people who sit unarmed and in complete nonviolence in front of the installations of destruction.

In these trials of the peace movement an attempt is being made to conceal the truth about what it is that threatens us and that is already killing other people. The judgments of the court up to now show how the motive is separated from the doer and the reasons for the action are ignored. Thus the application of the law is separated from the determination of truth, so that the law does not get involved with the truth. Why is the real crime, the arms buildup, the destruction of life that these same armaments supporters are carrying out every day, not the subject of debate here? Why are they trying to make criminals of us who are bringing this crime to light? Why is there no room in your mind, Your Honor, for something that, while not permitted—

such as blockading and obstructing—is still far from being a crime? Why don't you understand nonviolence? Are you so full of the violence to which you have submitted yourself that you can no longer see any action that stands apart from violence?

I want to remind you at this time of the great traditions of nonviolent action that are so little known in our country that our courts have to twist them into abomination and supposed violence.

As I was sitting in front of the works for mass destruction on Hiroshima Day, I thought about a simple woman, a textile worker from Montgomery, Alabama, who one day in December 1955 became a lawbreaker as she was taking the bus home. This black woman sat down in one of the seats in the bus that were supposed to be vacated for whites when called for. In the back, where the blacks belonged, there were no empty seats. And because she was tired, she went up front. When the bus driver ordered her to get up, she remained seated. Three other Blacks got up to make room for her. But Rosa Parks— that was the woman's name—remained seated even after a second order; the police were called and she was arrested. After this, the blacks organized a bus boycott that lasted 382 days; one of its leaders was a young pastor named Martin Luther King, Jr.

All of us today are looking for a way that will lead us out of the circle of violence and subjugation, injustice and the acceptance of it, crime and complicity. For Rosa Parks, the situation had become unbearable. I imagine that she had swollen feet and simply could not stand up for another three-quarters of an hour. Rosa Parks had worked as a secretary in a black organization. The legal means for opposing discrimination against and humiliation of blacks were exhausted. It had been of no use. And so it is with us who regard the arms buildup as a crime.

What can we, who are still a minority, do to stop the madness? Experience has shown that hoping for electoral victories and for a gradual change in parliaments and legislatures cannot be reconciled with the hope for peace. What other means, then, are at our disposal for acting against this crime? What is the role of the conscious minorities to which we belong?

An American, Henry Thoreau, is regarded as the spiritual father of civil disobedience. He lived during the time of slavery, and he considered what democrats could do when the majority in the country were still in favor of slavery—which, after all, was an advantageous and convenient institution for many; when only a conscious minority understood slavery as the crime that it is. What should the minority do? Was it enough to wait for the next election? Thoreau regarded this acceptance of injustice as unworthy of free men and women, and he called for passive resistance, for noncooperation, for civil disobedience. Thus, the question involved in the resistance of conscious minorities against majorities is essentially whether there are sociopolitical issues that may not be decided by elections, even free elections. Thoreau and his many successors have always answered this question in the affirmative when it is a matter of human dignity, which is also regarded by our constitution as inviolable. And human dignity is the central stake in the question of slavery, as also in the question of preparations for war.

Many American Christians in the peace movement have also compared our present situation with slavery. We are still blackmailing other people with atomic slavery, with nuclear destruction of all life; we are still allowing ourselves to be enslaved by the logic of madness. We are living in a transitional period at present; the majority still believe in war as the last resort, and only a conscious minority understand that the arms buildup is a crime. How can this minority of conscience bring the majority over to their side, so that gradually everyone will realize that the acquisition of armaments does not solve any problems, but instead threatens the lives of all of us on this little planet Earth? When will we be rid of this form of slavery, when will war be just as unthinkable for us as slavery, when will we stop planning and preparing for it?

Thoreau was a very democratic thinker. He did not believe that the American government would lock up thousands of people like prisoners of war; he thought that the moral power of the minority was stronger than the indolence of the majority. He thought that a democratic government was obligated not only to enforce formal laws, but was also called on to create justice and to make peace. He called the conscious minority to visible resistance, to the breaking of rules and police orders, to illegality. He believed that a government could not stand for long without the conscious moral minority of its people.

Gandhi made the following thoughtful statement about himself in the days before he turned to nonviolence: "Being a coward, I clung to violence." I think that is the normal situation of all of us. As cowards, we cling to violence in a double sense: We believe in violence and we submit to it. We think that only violence can protect us—the violence of whipping, violent punishment, military violence, nuclear violence. As cowards, we submit to violence and think there is nothing we can do about it. I believe that millions of people have exactly the same feelings as we in the peace movement do about the arms race, about the warmongering speeches of Reagan and Weinberger, about the nation that has bombed Libya like a superterrorist. They feel just as much anxiety about the militarization of our country and the leaders who are planning megadeaths. But they have submitted to violence, and they live in a state of resignation. What can we do, anyway? We are dependent on the Americans; the little man or woman has nothing to say. That is what Gandhi meant when he said, "Being a coward, I clung to violence"—I trusted it, and I submitted to it.

We blockade the mass destruction bases because we no longer wish to submit to violence. Nonviolent action is an act of freedom—freedom to interrupt the circle of violence. One of the freest people I know is the nonviolent pacifist Daniel Berrigan. He is free to speak or to be silent in court; free to follow an order or to defy it; free to join others in disarming nuclear warheads, and free to go to prison. He has not been broken by long periods in jail; he has kept his smile, his patience, his efforts to entice others to nonviolence. It is a freedom that does not let itself be enslaved by the experiential knowledge that only violence makes us secure. In the Letter to the Romans we read: "Do not be conformed to this world but be transformed by the renewal of your mind" (12:2). Nothing characterizes the world today so thoroughly as its global militarization, the conviction that conflicts can only be solved and freedom can only be salvaged by war and the threat of destruction.

Prophets and pacifists express in all ages their protest against national caprice and their vision of a human future, not only in words, declarations, and appeals, but also through symbolic action. I am thinking of Jeremiah, who, standing in a public place, laid a yoke on his shoulders in order to demonstrate provocatively—today we would say, by obstructing traffic—the coming defeat of his nation (Jeremiah 28). Or take Ezekiel, who, in conscious contradiction of public opinion, anticipated the coming catastrophe in his external appearance by cutting the hair of his head and beard to demonstrate how his land would be shaved close by the Babylonian army (Ezekiel 5). And I am thinking especially of Jesus, who overstepped the most important religious and civil law, that of the Sabbath regulations. He plucked grain, because people around him were hungry; he healed sick people on the Sabbath, including some who had been lame or handicapped for many years and could just as well have waited until Monday—symbolic, provocative actions in defiance of law and convention. Jesus wanted, through these violations of the laws, to call attention to situations of injustice. In doing so, he represented a kind of counter-public opinion.

That is exactly what we have been practicing in the peace movement in recent years. We have learned that particular actions defy existing laws or rules—that is, they are illegal—but at the same time they can be carried out in a completely nonviolent manner on our part, and thus threaten no one. When the blacks in the civil rights movement went into a restaurant that was for whites only, they acted illegally. They were ignored, cursed, beaten, and thrown out, but maintained their nonviolence. The peace movement today is joining itself with these very experiences. Of course it is illegal to blockade a munitions truck; but is it violence? The people taking such actions represent our only hope, because they utter a clear NO to the ruling violence of militarism, the more and more gigantic arms buildup, and the repression of every voice that is raised against the mixture of preparations for killing and death.

And these people need patience and a new political culture that is characterized, among other things, by the exclusion of national violence and state terrorism, by rejection of the still common forms of Stone Age relationships, rejection of what is traditionally called war—although we really need a different terminology, because we have no more "weapons," only means of mass destruction. The Nazis did not call the gas they used in Auschwitz a "weapon," either. And the people who are carrying out their planning games with the present means of mass destruction are criminals. Even those who only identify themselves in a hidden manner with death, cooperating and conforming, are destroying their own lives; they are not alive even now.

This new culture must be saturated with a deep love of life. I sense, in an apocalyptic despair that stares like someone mesmerized at the coming catastrophe, without yet perceiving the struggle and the argument, a kind of devastation, cynicism, and contempt for humanity. People need hope for the struggle. They have to think that conversion, such as that of Franz Alt,[1] is possible. The hope that the blind will see and the deaf hear is called, in religious language, faith—faith in people's ability to be changed by the experience of love and justice. The hope that the desire for death and murder is not the ultimate thing that inspires people; the certainty of a life force that is also in other people, in my political foes, and that is not exhausted when I am—that is God.

Why do you want to make criminals of these young people who are an expression of our country's greatest hope? Today we can determine objectively that the analyses and prognoses of the peace movement were correct, and they are widely confirmed, even within the conservative camp. We in the peace movement have shown that the medium-range missiles were not stationed because of the Soviet SS-20s but independently of them, in order to maintain the "dominance of escalation," as you can now read in the *Frankfurter Allgemeine Zeitung*.[2] The "truth about the zero option"[3] is, according to the same newspaper, that the West *never* wanted it; it was only introduced as a propaganda ploy. In the same article, the expression "double resolution," which was supposed to make us believe in a Western interest in negotiations, is replaced by the clear expression "resolution to station," and Gorbachev's suggestion that all European nuclear weapons be eliminated by the year 2000 is rejected from the outset as too dangerous.

Today, now that the goals of the Strategic Defense Initiative have been clearly defined, we understand better than ever what our first-strike weapons are for. When the United States, or at least part of its population, and all its destructive potential have been made invulnerable, then the European weapons can be employed at any moment; Russian retaliation will only strike Europe. Protection for the United States and an increase of offensive weapons in Europe—those are the declared goals of the superpower that rules over us.

Is German justice being employed as a bailiff for these rulers? Do you really believe that you can extinguish the spirit of resistance, the longing for a peace that is built not on state terror and militarism, but on economic justice, the power of the Spirit who consoles and encourages us? I am happy to be living in these times, when so much resistance is arising against the system of violence and national-militaristic terror. I am proud of the young people who are being persecuted today for the cause of justice and who are imprisoned for the cause of peace. They are in prison for all of us in the hope that one day our country will again be capable of peace. That is what we are fighting and working for. You are still trying to intimidate and deter us, but we will not give up our goal of making our land a place for peace once again. You can condemn us, but you cannot silence women like me and my sisters, you cannot extinguish us. It is like trying to forbid the roses to bloom. But the White Rose of resistance is blooming today, here in West Germany.[4]

Notes

1. The Catholic journalist Franz Alt became an outspoken proponent of the peace movement and proposed application of the Sermon on the Mount to politics. His television show was forced off the air.

2. *Frankfurter Allgemeine Zeitung,* 22 February 1986.

3. The U.S. proposed the removal of all SS-20s and other missiles aimed at western Europe as the price for *not* stationing its own Pershing and Cruise, but refused to make British, French, or German missiles part of the equation.

4. See Inge Scholl, *The White Rose,* trans. Arthur R. Schultz, intro. by Dorothee Sölle, 2d ed. (Middletown, Conn.: Wesleyan University Press, 1983).

PART TWO

God, Mother of Us All

God and Her Friends

When the Russian cosmonauts returned from space, they were asked whether they had seen God. And then, so goes this lovely story, they first fended off their questioners and refused to answer, saying, "No, no, we don't want to talk about that." Until finally a persistent journalist came along and questioned one of the cosmonauts very closely: "Now tell us: you saw something. What was it?" Then came the wonderful answer: "Yes, but don't tell anyone. She's black. God exists! She's black!"

This is a joke on several levels: on the first level, because atheistic white men suddenly discover something that is completely different from them, namely, black and a woman. It is a theological, racist, and sexist joke, if you will. It calls attention to the fact that Western theology is normally racist, that is, that it thinks white, and that it is sexist as well—both of these mostly on the unconscious level. We have no real idea of the power of the images that dwell in us, that as a matter of course and unquestioningly represent God as a white man, so we are shocked by the idea: "she's black."

Feminist theology has something in common with the German Democratic Republic: quite a few people think it necessary to precede anything said about either of them with the word "so-called." By means of this defense mechanism they try to keep their distance from reality, as if what feminist theologians do is not theology in any authentic sense and is more a kind of linguistic fad. I think that is a dangerous mistake. The awakening of a new religious consciousness on the part of women inside and outside organized religion is an event of the highest importance in the history of the churches. The World Council of Churches held a consultation in Sheffield, England, in July 1981, under the title "The Community of Women and Men in the Church." This consultation articulated some new questions. In a summary letter to the member churches we read: "In churches and societies that have been dominated by men, to the great detriment of women, and of men as well, we need both repentance and trust, in order to set out in obedience to God's call in the Gospel."[1]

Feminist theology belongs in the broad context of present-day theology that understands itself under the heading of liberation theology. This *liberación* grows out of an ecumenical, worldwide movement of Christians who are no longer prepared to reconcile or mediate existing world injustice through theology and faith; who no longer permit themselves to cover up injustice or to project it theologically onto a higher plane. The gospel challenges us to act provocatively, to uncover and attack injustice, to struggle against what is. Liberation theology is "critical" in this sense. It expressed itself in its European predecessors as critical, not affirmative, theology; as political theology, and not one that thinks it possible to say almost anything "theologically" and so be apolitical; and now as feminist theology that cannot deny the sexism that dominates us.

We need repentance, both by the oppressors and by those who have allowed themselves to be oppressed so long. All these expressions that we use to describe theology contain a critique of the notion of an apolitical theology and of the almost completely unconscious sexism the notion contains. Sexism, a word modeled on *racism*, means a way of speaking, thinking, and acting in which one sex, singled out solely because of its gender characteristics, is condemned and deprived.

Liberation theology, which is the milieu of feminist theology, begins with a new translation of the Greek word *soteria*, which originally had the meaning of rescue from life-threatening danger, from prison, from shipwreck, etc. It has traditionally been translated "salvation" or "redemption," but now it is interpreted as "liberation." Salvation is liberation, Christ is the liberator. His message about the reign of God is understood as the announcement of the building up of a world in which justice and, consequently, peace will be possible. The liberator in this context does not descend vertically from above as one who transports us from a bad situation to a better one, as salvation is often understood. Instead, he is the representative of the liberation movements of people who work to free themselves. In his spirit and with his strength to aid them, they have entered into the process of liberation.

It is important to understand this point clearly. While salvation is only the deed of someone who is wholly other, for the benefit of the saved, liberation is understood as a kind of cooperation between Christ and human persons. In this sense liberation theology has a certain anti-Protestant thrust, because this cooperation contradicts the traditional Protestant principle of *sola gratia,* grace alone. Liberation cannot be granted as a gift of grace that someone gives to another. Neither peoples, social classes, nor the oppressed portion of humanity can be given liberation in the absence of efforts on the part of those concerned to achieve that liberation. The concept of liberation presupposes participation in struggle. Mao Zedong not only said, "Women hold up half the sky," but added, "and they must conquer it."

We often misunderstand liberation as a wholly one-dimensional politico-economic matter. I want to emphasize, in opposition to that misconception, and precisely in the feminist theological sense, the multidimensionality of liberation. We consider liberation to be an event or process that cannot be understood simply in economic terms because it has many dimensions. One basic symbol of liberation theology is the exodus of the people of Israel from Egypt. The exodus has an economic dimension: these were slaves who had been ordered to make a double measure of bricks; that is, their wages were cut in half. The exodus has a political dimension: an oppressed people found its unity in its national leader, Moses, and so escaped from slavery. It has a social dimension: this people grew together in the course of the struggle for liberation. It has a psychological and cultural function: the Israelites discovered that they could not sing the songs of their God under oppression in Egypt, because in that culture of injustice even their religion was injured. In this sense the exodus also has a religious dimension: "Coming out" is a current version of the exodus theme, as homosexual women and men openly acknowledge their difference and walk out of the prison of tacit connivance.

Liberating events are multidimensional. On this point I want to tell one anecdote from Nicaragua. It is about a woman who can show us a little of what liberation means today. Reporters come into a small village where the literacy campaign has been going on. An old woman, about seventy, is standing there and a reporter asks her, "Can you read?" She looks at him, grins, and says very slowly, "Not yet." Liberation has many dimensions, and precisely this one—that people who were regarded in our society as superfluous and useless suddenly get the chance to learn something, even if it has no further economic value—is a cultural-religious dimension.

I understand feminism as the conscious part of the women's movement that struggles not only for equal rights, but for a new and different culture. The middle-class women's movement fights for equal rights, and this is part of the whole women's struggle. Of course it would be wonderful if women could play in the Berlin Philharmonic; if at the SALT-II negotiations women not only made coffee and typed manuscripts, but joined in the consultations. Those are good and desirable goals, toward which the middle-class women's movement is working. But we understand feminism to be something more, namely, that we go beyond the big *and* to a big *other*. We mean by this that the culture in which we are living now is false, because it injures, destroys, and cripples people and thereby prevents them from becoming full human beings. Feminist goals and values must be different from the dominant male goals and values.

Men are also involved in this liberation movement. In the American discussion of feminism there appeared, more than ten years ago, an essay that asked: "Was Jesus a Feminist?" The author, Leonard Swidler, gave an affirmative answer, supported by relatively good arguments drawn from the New Testament. One need not be a woman in order to be a feminist. There are enlightened, sensitive men who understand women's struggle, support it, take part in it, and in this sense are also to be called feminists—and who call themselves feminists if they have courage enough. Feminism, then, is not a kind of racism in which one part of humanity is defined or treated the way women have been defined and treated, namely, as nonhuman beings. Feminism is an attempt to articulate the battle between the sexes in such a way that the oppressors can also be winners. If Jesus was a feminist, in contradiction to the patriarchal culture that surrounded him, then why not some of today's men too?

A song from the American women's movement, a kind of prayer, says, "Make me strong, keep me weak, Mother Goddess." This text is not simply a prayer for strength, for the big *and*, but a prayer for the big *other*, for the will to remain weak. That means that as a woman, as a feminist, I do not want to become a man; I do not want the advantages, the privileges, the blindness, the career that a man has. That does not interest me at all. The goal of the women's movement is not becoming vice president of General Motors, as one American woman expressed it well; instead, it is to change the system in which General Motors has a president and vice president, so that maybe we don't need such people at all. So I want to remain weak; that is, I do not want to achieve some supposed strength. I do not want to surrender my identity, I do not wish to learn to define myself in this way as independent. How could I want a "God" whose highest attributes were independence, aseity, and omnipotence? A God who needs no friends?

Feminist theology needs new subjects to carry it on. My American women friends have often asked me: What does your theology have to do with your being a woman? I had never asked myself that question in Germany. It never came up during my studies. In the lectures I heard, Augustine had no skin color; no one seriously asked whether he was black or white. We thought it made no difference. In fact, I am more and more deeply persuaded that it makes a great deal of difference whether a theologian lives in a slum or in a villa. It makes a difference what sex a theologian is. It makes a difference what color skin she or he has. That consciousness is very lively in all liberation theologians; we summarize it in the concept of "contextuality." The context is decisive and must be critically analyzed before the "text," the traditional element, can speak.

Black people today, the world over, are asking: What do we need with a Christ who is the color of the oppressors? The whites have only white ideas in their heads. What good are they to us? Poor Christians in Latin America ask: How can the gringos teach us theology? Women ask: What do we need with a God whose most important quality stands for nothing more than the masculine ideal, namely, having power? The exodus from each Egypt of oppression, the withdrawal from these Egyptian fleshpots, means that people separate themselves from the given culture. It means that blacks leave behind the opportunities that the black bourgeoisie has in America today; that women leave their marital cages; that elite educational establishments are seen as less important than the goal of providing an education for everyone. If we suppose that the theology from which we can learn the most is being done by those who are making the exodus, and not by the Egyptians, then a theology comes into being that is not transported from above downward, but that arises from below. It no longer reflects domination but liberation, liberation from the colonialism under which we live.

Most women within sexist society are colonialized. Their consciousness has not remained unaffected by what has been done to them. Let me give a personal example. Two girls told me that they had hitchhiked alone through France. They were so young that all my motherly instincts awoke and I thought: but you can't do that, it is much too dangerous, God knows what can happen! As I stammered that out, they explained to me how wrong it is always to think first of the dangers threatening a woman, how impossible it is to let this society dictate everything to us, to let the night be taken away from us—to prevent us from going for a walk at night, hitchhiking, just living the way we want to—and instead to let ourselves be confined by atrocious rules of caution. While I was talking with them, I thought of the time when I was their age and remembered my internalized fears, and how little I had considered what an enslavement it was not to be able to do certain things because, as a woman, I was constantly afraid, brought up to be afraid, a colonialized being.

The concept of colonialization comes from Franz Fanon's *The Wretched of the Earth*. The colonial lord invades the country of the women and even provides them with the ideas according to which they are to live. For the majority of women in our country that still involves a narrowing of their interests, a kind of compulsive familialism. Family is everything to them and is compulsorily taught, encouraged, culturally and religiously undergirded. A woman is seen in relation to the family and comes to think of herself in that context; she doesn't want anything else, she has no other interests. Of course, she sometimes thinks, after the children have left home or when some other crisis arises, that maybe that was not the right choice of a life, that a person really cannot live solely for the family home and for this kind of nuclear family. But those are only passing suspicions; they either go away, or else the woman goes to pieces inside.

There is a kind of artificial stupification that goes with colonialism, an internalizing of the oppressor, a surrender of the possibility of self-determination. I think that female piety very often partakes of this kind of Uncle Tom character. As the black movement has freed itself from the Uncle Toms because they represented the slave state—suffering, good-natured, passive—so the women's movement has to free itself from those who, suffering, accepting, encased in an ideology of sacrifice, accept the idea that being a woman means being excluded from normal ways of living. The goal is the self-realization of full humanity in which particular characteristics, abilities, and experiences are not excluded at the outset.

What does it mean when new subjects enter theology, people who live and think out of different backgrounds and other contexts from those who have been in theology heretofore? Will not their theology change as well? First there is the material-biological existence we live. It really does make a difference whether I am a woman or a man. It makes a difference for my thinking, feeling, the way I do theology, the way I want to live with others, the kind of religious culture I and others want to build. The influence of women in the basic communities that have arisen in Latin America and in Europe, for example, is quite typical. The democratizing of the meaning of community, church, and religious fulfillment does not proceed downward from above, but really upward from below. And among those "below" are women who have had distinctly female experiences, which they contribute and no longer conceal. Some of these experiences arise from our biological existence, which we must take seriously. It is important not to deny that. I have to be aware that I think differently because I am a woman and have experiences such as menstruation; or, to bring it from the biological to the social level, because I have experiences such as being terribly ashamed because I have a spot on my dress. These primitive biological experiences are part of my life. I do not want to keep them separate from theology. I am not interested in doing abstract, exalted, idealistic theology. I want "head and belly," as we say. Bodiliness is something we must not suppress, trivialize, ignore, or conceal in shame. The remnants of Platonizing idealism in Christianity must be overcome.

In this way we learn to think materialistically, and that is an attempt to dissolve the divisions that we in the West have adopted—between spirit and matter, nature and spirit, body and soul, here and hereafter—and to formulate a critique of these divisions. For all of them have always contained the meaning expressed in the West's formula of domination: *divide et impera*—divide and conquer. First you separate everything into the natural and the spiritual, and then this division is used to facilitate domination, rule, superiority, and discrimination. "Divide" has been used in the sexist sense. Men have identified the so-called feminine with "nature," with the "bodily," the "instinctual," with a certain natural gift that men partly fear and partly hope to control. In any case, the separation has been used to put women in second place: *le deuxième sexe*.

One thing to notice about the new subjects doing theology is their consciousness of economic structures and forces. If we take these new people seriously, we have to take their economic situation into account. The most powerful examples of liberation theology in Latin America come from the pastors, nuns, priests, and even from higher dignitaries in the hierarchy who took their departure from just that symbolic point of wealth and more or less abandoned their palaces. They moved out, like Giovanni Franzoni in Rome or Don Mazzi in Florence. They moved from the huge, stony palazzi of the late Middle Ages and early modern era, into a different context, to live with the people they work with. This economic connection is just as important as the biological and involves a change in the subjects themselves.

Within the women's movement there is a new interest in how individual persons develop and become damaged; a concern with working through one's life history, one's psychosexual history. This expansion of consciousness through exploration of one's own history, this new subjectivity, is also transferred to theology.

Let me give an example of how theology can change when women do it; that is, when new subjects reflect on theological tradition. Sin, in the dominant, Protestant-influenced interpretation, is "wanting to be like God." It is the search for power, for superiority; it is overestimation of the self; it is pride; it is disobedience. But women who have become aware of their situation and have asked themselves, for the first time, whether they would really consider this type of sin to be the worst of all have come to quite different conclusions. They have said it is just the opposite. Our sin is not that of self-exaltation and pride; it is self-denial, selflessness in the bad sense of the word, the surrender of any kind of genuine self, underdevelopment of the self, conformity to the dominant structure, lack of pride in being a woman, obedience. Sin is submission to this sexist model of society. It is failure to realize God's image in oneself, and bowing in fearful obedience before institutions and traditions, conforming, practicing humility. That means that we need a totally different definition of sin if we want to talk seriously about the ways in which *we* mess up our lives and how *women* are destroyed in our society, how it happens that they never really come to life, and what is the source of all that.

The Protestant theologian Friedrich Schleiermacher, a romantic feminist, said in his ten commandments: "You shall not give false witness for the men, you shall not cover up their barbarity by your words and deeds." This expresses for me what I believe to be one of the key duties of women: to oppose the barbarity of the growing militarization of society—here, today.

A second point concerns the new objects of theology. Women are becoming a topic in theology. In her inaugural lecture at Union Theological Seminary, Old Testament scholar Phyllis Trible told a story from Judges 11:29-40. It is the story of Jephtha's daughter. (The girl has no name of her own.) Her father begs God for success in battle and in return promises to sacrifice the first thing that comes to meet him when he returns home. This is an ancient motif in fairy tales. When it is his only and beloved daughter who runs to meet him, he is obligated to sacrifice her. While he cries and laments, his daughter encourages him to keep his promise. Then she spends some time with her woman companions on a mountain before she is killed. Later, the daughters of Israel go out for four days every year to lament for Jephtha's daughter.

Although I have a very thorough knowledge of the Bible, I did not know this story, because it was never discussed, never brought up. This story stands in marked contrast to another Old Testament story about the sacrifice of a child, that of Isaac. The notable contrast is not only the missing name of the female child, but also the missing angel. No angel comes to change the ritual for Jephtha's daughter; she is slaughtered. It is a sad, bitter, hard story, and it has been interpreted as the story of women: a history of pain, of being forgotten, of being destroyed; no angel came. Women might be remembered in the cult, but essentially the salvation history of the people was not attached to them.

I believe that women who work in the women's movement, especially those who are concerned with religious renewal, dare not leave the history of pain, destruction, and forgottenness untouched. We have to think more about it, we have to remember such stories and understand them—I might say that we have to stand up for those who went before us, in order to make the overlooked stories live again.

In this sense—and this is a second example of the new objects of theology—we must reflect again on symbols for God, on the symbols we need in order to talk about God. I think that every person who cannot be a biological father—that is, every woman—has a different relationship to God the Father than do men, who can identify with the male image of God even if they renounce actual fatherhood. There are a great many social and psychological questions, including those of depth psychology, that need to be addressed in regard to the father-symbol for God.

My first question is, Why do people worship a God whose out-standing attribute is power, whose interest is in subjugating others, whose fear is that others could become his equal and somehow be like him; a being who is addressed as Lord and for whom mere power is not enough, so that his theologians have to credit him with om-nipotence? Why has this symbolic world become so well defined, why was it so important for those who reflected on it? What fantasies are behind it? Am I going too far when I call them "phallocratic fantasies," that is, the adoration of power?

And why should we women worship and love a being who does not transcend the moral level of present, male-determined culture, but only stabilizes it? I have asked myself: How could I desire to make power the central category of my life? How could I worship a God who is not greater than a man? When I was a young teacher, I always wished that I could at least shout loudly. I felt that I was incompetent because I could not do that, and I envied the men who had louder voices. In the meantime I have stopped envying them on that account. But I still associate with male power the ability to roar, the ability to give orders, to fire a weapon—all those specifically male character-istics. In this I do not think that I have been more injured by patriarchal culture than others. I am simply expressing what thousands of other women have more or less vividly experienced. I have realized more and more that this identification with the aggressor, with the mighty, with the rapist, this declaring-oneself-in-agreement with all of that power, is the most terrible misfortune that can happen to any woman.

Here I want to insert some remarks on method. When you study theology it is important to understand that all our God-language has symbolic character, and thus that there are very different ways of talking about God, so that you really cannot say that God *is* father, as if the two were identical. That means that every symbol that sets itself up as an absolute has to be relativized. God is really greater than our talk about God, greater than any of our languages. We have to be aware of that, because otherwise we will lock ourselves into sym-bolic prisons.

I find it to be one of the liberating functions of feminist God-talk that these symbolic prisons of patriarchy are being relativized, so that a ray of liberation shines through—for example, in the school in New York where I teach, when the Our Father is normally prayed as "Our Father and Mother in heaven." That always causes me to reflect on the relativity of our language and its symbols. I agree that "father" is one way to talk about God, but when it becomes the one compulsory way to talk, this symbol becomes a prison for God, and all the other symbolic language that people have used to express their experience of God is suppressed by the required language, or is forced onto a lower hierarchical level.

I do not think that we can solve the problem by thinking of God as father and supplementing power with mercy, the second characteristic of a father. That makes of God a kind of benevolent slaveowner who is loved and revered by his slaves. And in this sense it remains a spirituality without an exit, without an exodus. It would still be subjection for women to accept their roles in obedience to this God who supposedly has determined certain rules for them by nature. This is still destructive of our opportunities to be full human beings. The question is really whether the father symbol represents what we mean when we say "God," when we think of God in connection with liberation. "May God bless and protect you. May she let her face shine upon you and give you peace," said women in a worship service in St. Catharine's Church in Hamburg. "Our Father and Mother in heaven," many women in the ecumenical movement pray. Do we have to think of God as male?

These are examples of tentative efforts that are being made everywhere today where women have become aware of their situation. The desire for another conception of God, other symbols and other hopes, is important for those who need a different God because they are insulted, humiliated, and disgusted by the culture in which we live and think. After all, it is not primarily men who suffer from the sexism in theological language, but women, who feel themselves excluded, negated, unformulated, and silenced. In this connection, I think that the relativizing of a God-symbol that has been absolutized, such as the father-symbol, is only a minimum demand. Another possible way to attack the problem—and this is happening now in feminist theology—is to try different symbols. We can address God as Mother or Sister, if we want to remain in the realm of family language. We can also use symbols drawn from nature, which have the advantage of carrying a less authoritarian flavor, so that they may bring us closer to a theological language free of dominance. If I say that God is light or the sea, or the fountain of all good things, or living wind, those are symbolic efforts, words that are free from authoritarian overtones and for that reason are more appealing.

I think we can learn a great deal from mysticism in our search for a new language that expresses our relationship to God more clearly, less repressively, and with less danger of misunderstanding. Mysticism offers God-symbols without authority or power, thus without a chauvinistic flavor. The recognition of the higher power, the adoration of domination, the denial of one's own strength, have no place in mystical piety. There the relationship of master and slave is often explicitly criticized; more particularly, it is overcome through creative language. Religion, for mystics, is sensitivity, union with the whole; belonging, not subjection. People adore God not because of God's power and glory; instead, they sink into God's love, which is called ground, or depth, or ocean.

Coming to my last point, I want to say something about changing method in theology, in connection with the search for a new language. If we speak subjectively instead of trying to objectivize, we speak differently. If we do not silence the I and its experiences, if we do not learn to avoid the word "I" in a scholarly paper, we learn to express ourselves differently and at the same time to do a different kind of theology. The expulsion of women from theology not only affects the 51 percent of humanity who have remained theologically silent in the West, but it also has catastrophic consequences for the other 49 percent—the men—and for their language. The suppression of the feminine part of the soul—that is, the subordination of everything that smells like woman—has done more damage to theologians' language than anything in the secular world. It is not what comes from outside that is dangerous, or what is rationalistic or enlightened or otherwise tends to make God superfluous, but rather the destruction that men have brought on themselves by cutting off women and cutting out the woman in themselves. This mutilation of men plays a substantial role in the world of theology.

What took place was a process of purification and at the same time of impoverishment, when an emphatic, comprehensive, conscious, and integrative language was gradually and increasingly silenced. What a difference between theological books and the gospel! What a terrible discrepancy in their very different language! So-called scientific theology is normally an unconscious speech—that is, it is unaware of emotion, insensible to human experience, expressing a kind of ghostly neutralism without interests and without invitation, with no desire to be effectual. It is flat because in most theological language the shadow side of faith, which is doubt, has no place and is not admitted. But if we never say anything other than what we think in our heads, and never, never admit what contrary things we might have in our hearts, our language remains flat and slick, as theological language mostly is.

If you read male theologians' commentaries—say, on Eve's dialogue with the serpent in Paradise—you can see how sexual curiosity is damned in principle, and how an enormous fear of woman, of this curiosity, of this desire to begin something new, permeates the whole. The basic recurring feeling you get from these theologians is: Who would talk to a snake, anyway? Nobody would ever do such a thing as Eve did! The pervasive sexism of the theology is obvious. This kind of language, which increasingly excludes female participation and engages in a kind of scientizing that I consider extremely dangerous, really ends by destroying the language that theology needs: words that can touch human beings. Such a language grows out of experience and practice and leads us toward becoming different and acting differently.

Scientific theology attains this quality of living language very seldom, and then almost against its own will. It requires a certain talent for subversion for male theologians to achieve this kind of language, one might say in resistance to prescribed canons of scholarship that are oriented to these ideals of neutralism, of nonpartisanship, of freedom from emotion, and whose whole energy is directed to making the subject disappear. The rediscovery of a conscious, subjective language rich in emotion would be an appropriate task for a new theology. It would have to proceed inductively, not deductively, which means to begin with our experiences—not with statements about God, Scripture, dogma, or tradition—but with the daily events in our life that need to be theologically reflected upon, interpreted, and confronted.

An ordinary statement in the newspaper, like "The cosmetic industry was able to increase its sales in this area by 150 percent in recent years," is a piece of news. Doing feminist theology means understanding such a statement in all its dimensions: What really happened to people? Whose interests are being articulated here? What do we learn about life, about the quality of life?

Doing experiential, inductive theology seems to me very important in contrast to the deductivist tendency of previous theology. Feminist faith and theology understand praxis as the first step, theory and theology as a second, reflexive step. It is a general principle of liberation theology, as developed by Gustavo Gutiérrez, that one does not begin with theology but with faith. The traditional relationship of theory and practice has to be reversed. The hierarchical order in which theory or brainwork, mostly created by men, is the finer thing, while praxis is left for the common people, the women, the secretaries, is a destructive division of labor. Feminist theology in its methodology calls on other abilities besides abstraction and synopsis. Its interest is not in creating new dogmas but in narration, in telling. Narrative theology is a methodic expression of this new consciousness, namely, that we understand certain things more clearly, in more dimensions, more really; we get them under our skin when we tell them instead of reducing them, so to speak, to concepts. Therefore this element of narrative is extraordinarily important for the women's movement.

American women have a wordplay about this that scandalizes humanistically educated people: they say that we do not need *his*tory, but *her*story. We also need it when we try to tell the story of God with us, the story of God and her friends.

Note

1. Constance F. Parvey, ed., *The Community of Women and Men in the Church: A Report of the World Council of Churches' Conference, Sheffield, England, 1981* (Geneva: World Council of Churches, 1983).

Hope Springs from Below

It is generally the case, in the church and in the faith, that women are invisible and have been made inaudible. Even when they say something, nobody listens; they are only women, so what they say is nothing important, it doesn't count. And therefore the history of women in the church is also unknown.

This recently dawned on me as I was reading a new book on women's part in the struggle within the church and in the history of the Confessing Church. I learned there that the few women who then were pastors were almost all on the side of right, that is, not on the side of the German Christians, but in the Confessing Church. And that is really quite interesting. In this sense there were certainly enough women witnesses who could demonstrate how women took a stand against the dominant tendencies.

Therefore I consider the opinion that there simply are not and have not been any active women in the church to be a sexist phenomenon, one that I encounter everywhere in society and politics as well. There are always some liberal men who are delighted to explain to me: Oh, we would like so much to include women, but unfortunately there are no women judges anywhere in the world, no women doctors, no women heads of department, and there are certainly no women who are theologians. Well, of course, who would be surprised at that situation in this men's club? First discrimination is practiced and exercised, and then these liberals stare around their circle in aston- ishment and say: Oh, how remarkable—there are no women! First you create the situation that you later regard as a natural phenomenon, when in reality it was historically brought into being.

Regrettably, most of the testimony about the numberless women in the church and their activity is missing. History is written by the victors; we cannot say that often enough. That means that the losers, the oppressed, the blacks, the women, are not objects of history. The history books tell us about generals, great bishops, men who accom- plished something or other. But we know too little, for example, about women working in education, in the internal missions, in the effort finally to educate the members of the lower orders as well—efforts carried out by large numbers of women in the course of the great social movement of the nineteenth century. This represents a gap in research. Its consequence is that we think nothing happened and that women in those days just accepted everything the way it was. I simply don't believe that. We ought instead to begin with the working hy- pothesis that it just doesn't happen that people accept subjection, oppression, destruction of their own dignity in such numbers and without exception. That approaches the level of a theological question for me. In fact, I would consider it a kind of lack of faith in humanity to think that way, to think so disparagingly of women in particular, as if they had always been oppressed, willing to sacrifice, and still ready to prettify the whole business and never to rise up against it.

It took me quite a long time to understand how we women have been marginalized in this male society. I really did not intend to be a theologian in the professional sense; I wanted to be a teacher. I do not consider teaching a woman's fate or a job for women; it is really the most natural and most important profession a person can have. Everyone teaches something, otherwise she or he is not human. To that extent I am not at all unhappy about my choice. But it took a long time before I comprehended the discrimination in the university. At one time I thought I could teach at the university. But when I merely hinted at this once to a professor, he demanded to know how someone like me could ever get such a crazy idea. That was a big fiasco.

As a young teacher in a public school, I did not experience any specific discrimination, because this profession had always been strongly identified with women. Of course, it was also the case that most of our educational supervisors and directors were men who, because of the intellectual potential represented by the women in my postgraduate course, already felt a little unsure of themselves. They didn't act so triumphalistically male anymore.

It was only later, in the church, that I experienced overt sexism. I remember a little incident after the Church Congress in Cologne in 1965. I had given a talk that brought me a lot of recognition. Afterward, my other writings were more and more often published and disseminated. Then one day the Church Brotherhood of the Rhineland invited me to give a lecture. A friend told me later how, as I entered the lecture hall, one of the prominent men there said to his neighbor, nearly bursting with laughter, "Oh, she is tiny! Oh, God, how tiny she is!" He couldn't get over the fact that I wasn't six feet tall, that I didn't meet the principal criterion for a man. I mention that only because physical discrimination is part of sexism. It made clear to me how awful it really is, especially because no one would have said such a thing about a man of my rank or caliber, no matter how short he was. It is a basic trait of sexism to be unconscious. Men seldom think anything of it when they make the equation, quite as a matter of course: "The human being is a man. Period!" That is why we hear only talk about "brothers" all the time, and about "great men" in history.

I could recite a good many experiences to substantiate this widespread sexism. In the early years of my public activity I may have said or repeated—a little more sharply, perhaps more publicly, and with some conclusions—a good many things that I had learned, together with my fellow students of enlightened Lutheran theology of this century, especially from Rudolf Bultmann. Many others, many men, said the same things, but they never had as much trouble or received as many terrible letters as I did. After speaking to the Congress of the World Council of Churches in Vancouver in 1983, I received communications that often had a brutal sexist undertone; for example, "Why don't you go to Siberia, you old sow!" I got more of these fascist-sounding letters from men than from women, but there is a corresponding female hatred. Of course it hurts me, and it tells me something about the soul of my people when I see what kind of fearful hatred, nationalism, and sexism are surfacing there.

But happily, I have also had good experiences in connection with my many major disagreements and quarrels, and have gained wonderful friends. Quite a few people I did not know before have written to me and spontaneously taken my side. In the course of such episodes of hostility, many people have become so close to me that I was made increasingly conscious of an important truth: We who struggle against sexism, racism, and militarism belong together and are one group. I especially appreciated the words and action of one woman who, putting her arm around me, said: "You touched me. I want to touch you."

Certainly it is difficult for me to see a way out for some people who have written me such hate-filled letters, to suppose them still capable of learning. Very often they are older people with very hard-set, rigid outlooks or sensibilities. On the other hand, I think that at this very moment we have every reason to be grateful as we see how much has changed in our people as a result of and in the course of the peace movement. It is an enormous awakening involving millions—we were never so many as we are now. Therefore I have no reason for pessimism or enduring frustration. My difficulties, fears, hard knocks, and the buckets of mud thrown in my face—I have to acknowledge that—are undeniable, but I can by no means draw universal conclusions from them about the meanness of human beings in general or the Germans in particular. I am not bitter in that sense; in fact, I must honestly say that I am less and less so, because there are so many good experiences in the other direction. Of course the powers we are opposing are enormously strong: they are backed by billions of dollars, millions of cannon, thousands of generals, all of whom have no interest in seeing the world we dream of become a reality.

With regard especially to women and their disparagement, I think that the main reason for it is men's fear of women's power, of women who, once they get to the point of speaking, appearing in public, carrying out their goals—perhaps because they were oppressed so long—are less easily turned back or bought off. I think that a great many men, especially those who have positions of power and exercise functions of domination, have very deep fears of concentrated woman-power, in which emotion and rationality work together. Here the men have to contend not just against a head, but also against deep feelings. So often I hear some man or other tell me, "Don't be so emotional." Men think that is a dirty word. They are so broken that they don't even know how crippled they are. In their view of things, a person may not laugh or cry, be afraid or sad. He must run around with a stage mask in front of his face and express everything through a remarkable filter of rationality, which allows only very constricted and weak words to get through, speech that has no power to persuade, is devoid of any warmth and therefore must be accompanied by compulsion. Because they have no real power, they have to exercise "proper" authority: that is, the "authority" of administration, technical management, or finance. They have to dismiss people, oppress them, silence them, or shut them out. How can we change all that?

In the women's movement today we can distinguish a liberal and a feminist wing. The liberal wing works to obtain for us the rights that men already have—so that we can play in the Philharmonic, be heads of medical departments, and so on. That is a real and worthy goal, for without that I, for example, could not have gone to the university. Every reasonable person has to support this goal. We must only realize clearly that what women in the feminist wing of the women's movement want today is something more: We don't just want half the pie, we want a completely different pie from the one the men have been serving up to now.

To apply this to the church: We don't just want to bring systems of parity into the church now, so that half of the priests, pastors, superintendents, and bishops have to be women. That would be lovely, but it doesn't get us much further. Protestantism, which, with some exceptions, has admitted women to office for twenty or thirty years now, has already found this out. Nothing essential has changed in Protestantism as a result. It is still a pastors' church. Even if some of the people in the clerical robes are female, this has not worked to alter the institution. What we women really want is that the church should change, not just that we get more power in it. It ought to become a more human church, where certain forms of oppression and destruction of human beings no longer happen, where the gospel is lived in practice, where the principal aim is not to get along with the government and participate in its power, but really and truly to follow the poor man of Nazareth.

I think it is essential to be clear about the fact that we don't just want institutional power, because women's concern within the church is a theological or spiritual concern. We want a spirituality different from the one that continually says yes and amen, that is so obedient to the state that it cooperates in the increase of armaments or even lauds it (like the French bishops). We really want a different church, one that follows Jesus.

I once had a very interesting conversation with a Catholic sister in the United States about the ordination of women to the priesthood. This sister had been one of those who fought hard for this goal. I asked her: "How is it going, are you still at it?" And she said: "Do you know, I am not so sure anymore whether that is the most important thing. Because if the Pope were suddenly—which is unimaginable at the moment—but supposing the Holy Spirit would touch the Pope and enlighten him, and he would see that excluding half of humanity from the priesthood is contrary to the gospel, there is still the big question whether this image of the priest as we have developed it in the last two thousand years is not so strong that it would mold the women who would enter the priesthood in such a way that we really wouldn't have anything new and significantly different. That worries me a lot." This woman thought we should instead work subversively and from below—that is, in the places we have now, as pastoral assistants, for example, and by taking over the role of teachers in the church—so as to put across the content that really matters, even if it lacks institutional visibility for the moment.

I derive a good deal of optimism in this regard from my ecumenical experiences. I am not so sure about the church in Germany, because West Germany is a rather underdeveloped country in many respects—spiritually and theologically. On the other hand, the Christian feminism I have found in the ecumenical movement and in the United States is magnificent. I have had wonderful experiences with women who relate to one another and to tradition, to the Bible, to rituals—especially in the realm of liturgy and cult—in very different ways. The Christian women's movement has thus far not been very strong in feminist theology as an academic discipline; much more important has been what the Americans call "sister celebrations." Women celebrate liturgy with one another and in the process develop abilities quite different from men's. Here they break through mindless and empty piety and one-dimensional ritual. In all these liturgies there is one essential element: the participation of the individual women. Everyone takes part, everyone has something to offer. If we take it at a fundamental level, theologically speaking, it would always have to be that way, for no one can really do everything as proxy for others.

Today new and truly beautiful rituals are continually being created. One example: a Methodist woman in the United States was expelled from the church because she said publicly that she lived with another woman who was her lover. This woman had done good work and was very much loved by many people. We, as a group of women, held a kind of ceremony of mourning. There was a jug of wine and a large chalice on a table. Each of the women present went forward and expressed her sorrow, her pain, her anger, or perhaps her wishes, saying how shameful and wounding she felt this action to have been.

Then each woman poured a little wine into the chalice, which afterward was handed to all, so that in drinking we each took part in all that had been said. I find this a very fine example of participatory ritual.

I had another good experience in a seminar on feminism and piety where there were all kinds of tensions and difficulties. One woman suggested: "Let's stand up, hold hands, and be silent for a moment. Then let each one try to find a name for God, to say who God is for us." I cannot begin to describe how beautiful it was. I learned to know these people quite differently. One woman said, "Sister"; another, "The smile of my infant son in the morning when I lean over his crib, that is God." It was such a living devotion, and I understood again at depth what it is that really matters. Sometimes we can't see the forest for the trees, or God for the church.

Personally I am in favor of integration, in liturgy as well, so that men and women come together again. But I think that there is a necessary phase for many women in which they can do certain things only among sisters. A lot of women experience men, because of the male power roles, in such a way that the presence of men is a disturbing factor. I personally think that this is a transitional phase in secular as in Christian feminism. Women have first to become so strong together that they can later integrate again. But no one should ask that integration of them at the outset. First they have to develop their own life-styles and forms of expression. At this point in the history of the church, women need a kind of free space in which they can develop their own forms.

We cannot overlook the first successes. Thus, at a conference in Budapest on the theme, "Toward a Theology of Peace," four liturgies were planned, all to be led by men. When one of the men cancelled, a nun from the Philippines was asked to conduct the liturgy instead. It was so different, so beautiful, so warm, that everyone suddenly realized that the basic Protestant model (a hymn, a sermon, another hymn, finished) really was not enough and did not satisfy people. This woman had a completely different style, with a lot of participation—that is probably the decisive point—and much more expression of feeling, as well as silence. It isn't necessary to talk all the time. The whole thing was so persuasive—for the men there too—that we really have to say to men: It is almost incredible that anyone can simply shoo away or fence in the gift that women are now bringing to the altar—flowers, candles, songs, the content of their lives. To do so is blind and stupid and sick. For it is not as if we were asking for something; we are bringing something. Instead of being happy about it and saying, "Yes, amen, hallelujah—that's it!" they are afraid. That is so sinister that one really has to be afraid for men's reason and the health of their souls.

I don't want to appear too pessimistic in regard to our experiences here in West Germany. One measure of the way in which things are changing somewhat in the churches is surely the phenomenon of the semiannual church congresses (*Kirchentage*), as a form of mass movement and youth movement. And it is tremendous how much has changed in the Lutheran churches because of women, women's liturgies, women's days, the way women interpret the Bible, the way they speak a participatory language—that is, letting other people talk, not aiming at academic utterance, not trying to express themselves as artfully and unclearly as possible, but, on the contrary, bringing their own feelings with them and not denying them. This is already a new reality; without it, an institution like the German Lutheran Church Congress, for example, would not be imaginable.

Nor could we think of the church congresses now without the participation of young people. That is surely an encouraging phenomenon. Nevertheless, I think that the young people must also be encouraged to get involved in the institution, not simply in their own small groups. There is a strong tendency among them to slip into a corner or into their own niche. I can well understand that people need a niche like that, but I would like the niche to be in the big house of God, so to speak—there are churches with alcoves—where people could meet but still remain in relationship to the institution.

The greatest danger for young people is that they live with the feeling that there is no place at all for them: no place in the work world, no place in the university, no place in which to learn a trade— no place whatsoever, no air, no trees, nothing. I think it is dangerous when, out of this emotional reality of young people, there arises a generalized hatred of institutions, so that they think that when anything becomes an institution the spirit has left it and everything in it is dead. That is just a romantic mistake. Instead, we need to encourage young people to develop their own strength, to read the Bible together or to do certain actions in order to learn from them but also to enter consciously into conflict with the institution.

There is no sense in making a swing to the left, so to speak, and leaving the institution on the right. God knows, the institution is often terrible, rightist, and partly reactionary, but if we let it go on that way, we only advance its destruction and isolate ourselves. I have no time for that. I think that these struggles are necessary and that obviously it is the duty of those who want to change something to incite the struggles, for the big institution wants peace—the peace of the graveyard; it wants quiet and order. So the conflicts have to be swept under the rug. But in fact, it is our duty to say no and to stick to it, so that something will be changed and made better. The Christian tradition gives us enough examples of the necessity of such action.

Today the church from below is more spiritual and intellectually alive and active than the church from above. That is nowhere so clear as in the matter of nuclear armaments. Those are the kinds of struggles in which we are engaged and in which we are trying to push the leaders of the churches slowly in a clear, unequivocal direction, so that they will finally take sides, for the sake of the gospel—and not take the side of the party of death or even consider it possible to do so. That could be the most important task of the churches today: finally to dismiss these powers of death, to say no once and for all to the further plundering of the Third World, to the piling up of armaments, and the destruction of nature—the three principal deadly tendencies of society.

There are such things as ethical heresies, when people turn away from religion not because of some tenet of faith or other, but morally. And a large portion of the church is living in just this ethical heresy. It must be overcome. For me, the worst of all is that the churches, in West Germany also, repeatedly take the side of the rich against the poor, that they support the war of the rich against the poor by supporting armaments and consequently choose in favor of the nonsupport of those who are starving. Of course, they don't say so, but de facto that is what they do as a matter of course in their support of the neurotic babble about security and what follows from it, the endless increase of armaments.

I would very much like to believe that this development would have been different had women been in responsible positions, but of course there are justifiable objections to that idea. For example, it is always horrifying to think of Margaret Thatcher. There are women who have so denied and betrayed their womanhood that they no longer have any idea why they are women and what it means to be a woman. Nevertheless, I hope that we women in the church, if we act in greater numbers and greater solidarity, can change something. We can see this in the ecumenical church panels where more women are in charge or participate. These experiences give me hope for the church.

I want to close with a poem stemming from Nicaragua's experience, in which I was inspired by events there when the pope visited that little country. I think it was a historic event for the church when the pope was interrupted by women in Nicaragua.

Ernesto Cardenal tried in vain
to kiss the pope's hand

Why are you doing that, my brother
the hand that strikes you
and blesses our enemies
why do you bow so low
my unbending brother
and build up hope

my raped sister
the hope from below

The women in your country
have prepared themselves for a long time
for the visit of their holy father
when he did not speak to them
only about them
they broke in on the pope
and interrupted with peace

in the name of my raped sister
of the hope from below

So on a single day they broke
two walls
of centuries-old silence
that suffocates us from above
so they built more strongly than you
my unbending brother

my raped sister
the hope from below[1]

Note

1. Dorothee Sölle, *verrückt nach licht: gedichte* (Berlin: Fietkau, 1984).

Fatherhood, Power, and Barbarism

FEMINIST CHALLENGES TO AUTHORITARIAN RELIGION

One of the names of God in the Jewish-Christian tradition is Father. What are the practical implications of this symbolic name at the present time? I want to consider, not the history of the origins of the symbol, but the history of its effects; not the question "What was its original intent?" but rather "What happened to it?" And so I come to two theological realities: the Father-God and the culture of obedience. Both expressions cause me major difficulties, which I will formulate in three questions:

1. Has obedience produced and helped to shape a culture or a barbarism?
2. Can the word *father* still stand for God when we have learned to think of God and liberation as inseparable?
3. What elements of the father-symbol are indispensable?

These questions should not be dehistoricized or desubjectivized. I am posing them as a German, as a woman, and as someone who is trying to be a Christian at the end of the twentieth century, and I do not wish to deny my national, my sexual, or my socioeconomic identity. That makes it difficult, because the rules of theological language, while they know how to differentiate between the God of the philosophers and the God of Abraham, Isaac, and Jacob, are still ignorant of the God of Sarah, Rebecca, and Rachel. The fathers in faith are reduplicated in the father in heaven; the mothers of faith are still in the dark: prehistorical, unremembered, forgotten, and suppressed.

I. The Culture of Obedience and Barbarism

My oldest difficulty with a culture of obedience stems from my national identity. The history of my people is colored by a central event in this century that changed its language, ideas, conceptions, and images. Words and concepts have ineluctably acquired a different quality because of that event; they have lost their innocence. Precisely as someone who lives after that event and who deals with language, I cannot and I will not forget. In a particular text—a poem, for example— certain words carry their historical fate with them. *Star, smoke, hair* all still had in 1942 a different meaning in German from the one they have now, after the greatest crime and misery in the history of my people.

My first question to a "Christian culture of obedience" is whether obedience is not one of those ideas that can no longer remain intact after the Holocaust.[1] It is for historians to decide how much weight is to be given to Christian training in obedience in Germany as a preparation for fascism. For theologians, repeated references to obedience by Adolf Eichmann, whose parents had registered him in the YMCA, or by Rudolf Hess, whose father had marked him for a priest, are enough to rob the concept of its theological innocence. Nor does it help much to seek the most obvious way out by trying to distinguish between "genuine" or "proper" obedience to God and that owed to human beings. Can one ask for an attitude toward God and train people in that attitude while at the same time criticizing the same behavior toward people and institutions?

Must obedience lead to barbarism? This question should not be limited to historical fascism. Obedience today defines itself independently of charismatic leaders in terms of the so-called givens of economics, the consumption of energy and expanding militarism. The technocrats have long since inherited the mantle of the priests. But the structural elements of authoritarian religion remain, even in the new relations of obedience, although these prefer to disguise them-selves as merely the "rules of the game," and the relics of religious training prepare increasingly religionless people for an obedience from which all personal traits and any relationship to trust and self-surrender have vanished. The new, computerized obedience has three structural elements in common with the older religious type:

1. Recognition of a higher power that has our fate in its hands and excludes any self-determination.
2. Submission to the rule of this power, which needs no moral legitimation such as love or justice.
3. A deep pessimism about the human person: she/he is not ca-pable of love or truth, but is a powerless and meaningless being whose obedience feeds on the very denial of her or his own strength.

The cardinal virtue of authoritarian religion is obedience; the car-dinal sin is resistance—in contrast to a humanitarian religion, where the corresponding virtue and vice are, respectively, self-realization and misspent life.[2] In terms of social history, this kind of authoritarian religiosity functions to affirm the society and stabilize its dominant tendencies. Within authoritarian religion, emancipatory willingness to change and critical transcendence of what is are rejected, even and especially when they are religiously founded: God's justice and love are less important than God's power. Authoritarian religion reveals an infantile need for consolation that expresses itself aesthetically and in the history of piety as sentimentality; it is matched, however, by a compulsive need for order, fear of confusion and chaos, and a desire for comprehensibility and dominance. It is precisely its rigidity that outlasts the other moments of a dying religion; the authoritarian ties remain as part of the technocratic interpretation of life. The Milgram experiment, in which an overwhelming majority of ordinary people were prepared to torture innocent people with electric shocks at the direction of scientists, fits very well in the context of a culture of obedience. Obedience functions well within fascist or technocratic barbarism.

II. God and Liberation

Erich Fromm distinguished between humanitarian and authoritarian forms of religion. The historical Jesus, early Buddhism, and the mystics in most religions are examples of a nonrepressive religion that does not rest on one-sided, asymmetrical dependence or realize itself by means of internalized compulsion. It is precisely at this point that the sociopsychological questions about the father-symbol begin.

Why do people revere a God whose most important quality is power, whose interest is in subduing, who fears equality, a being who is addressed as Lord, for whom mere power is not enough, so that his theologians have to credit him with omnipotence? The most important question posed by a developing feminist theology to those in authority is directed against phallocratic fantasies, against the adoration of power. Why should we honor and love a being that does not transcend the moral level of a culture currently shaped by men, but instead serves to stabilize it?

To put it in terms of my own theological autobiography: My difficulties with the great and powerful arise out of the experience of Auschwitz. In 1965 I published my first book, *Stellvertretung. Ein Kapitel Theologie nach dem Tode Gottes.*[3] The position I defended there is radically Christocentric, in the tradition of Bonhoeffer. Godself, God as acting and speaking, cannot be experienced. We can relate to the powerless Christ who was independent of authority, who has nothing but his love with which to win and save us. His powerlessness is an inner authority; we are not his because he has begotten, created, or made us, but because his weaponless power is love, which is stronger than death.

My difficulties with the father, begetter, possessor of power, and determiner of history were deepened as I began to understand more clearly what it means to be born a woman—that is, "mutilated"— and to live in a patriarchal society. How could I wish to make power the central category in my life; how could I revere a God who is not more than a man? With male power I associate things like the ability to roar, giving orders, learning to shoot. I do not think that I in particular have been damaged by patriarchal culture more than other women. It has simply become more and more obvious to me that any identification with the aggressor, with the powerful, with the rapist, is the most terrible fate that can overtake any woman.

Nor does the father-symbol have the same fascination for those who can never be fathers. Even power combined with mercy, even the kind father, is not a solution for this problem. A good slaveowner may be loved and honored by his slaves; female piety is frequently a kind of Uncle Tom devotion. But submission to the roles defined as "feminine" and obedience to God, who has supposedly established these rules in our nature, destroy our chance to be full human beings. A father cannot free us from the history of my people or from the sexism of the ruling culture. Can the father-symbol still represent what we mean by the word *God*?

If we understand that we can only speak symbolically about God, every symbol that sets itself up as absolute must be relativized. God really transcends our talk about God, but only when we no longer lock God up in symbolic prisons. I can admit that "father" is one way of talking about God, but when it is made compulsory as the *only* way, the symbol becomes a prison for God. All the other symbolic expressions that people have used to describe their experience of God are repressed by the obligatory language or are demoted to a lower level in the hierarchy.

Pope John Paul I said, in a remark that has drawn a lot of attention, that God is at least as much mother as father. But in practical religious life we are still far behind this relativizing of the symbolic language. After a worship service in St. Catharine's Church in Hamburg that began "In the Name of the Father and the Mother, the Son and the Spirit," there was an excited discussion about whether one may speak that way. Changing sanctified liturgical language is one step outside the prison and therefore is felt as threatening. Four women gave the blessing together: "May God bless and protect you. May she let her face shine upon you and give you peace."

These are examples of tentative efforts that are being made everywhere today where women have become aware of their situation. The desire for another image of God, for new symbols and different hopes, is important for those who need a different God because they are insulted, humiliated, and disgusted by the culture in which we live. After all, it is not primarily men who suffer from the sexism of theological language.

The relativizing of a God-symbol, like "father," that has been used absolutely, is a minimal demand in this context. There are other symbols for God: we can say "mother" or "sister" to her, if we want to remain within the framework of family. However, I find that symbols drawn from nature are clearer, because of their nonauthoritarian quality. A theological language free of dominance can draw on the mystical tradition: "fountain of all goodness," "living wind," "water of life," "light" are all God-symbols without authority or power, without any chauvinist flavor. The recognition of the "higher power," the adoration of dominance, the denial of our own strength, have no place in mystical piety.

The master-slave relationship has often been expressly criticized, but it is especially the use of creative language that has made it outdated. Religion here is the experience of oneness with the whole, of belonging, not of submission. People do not worship God because of God's power and domination; they "sink" into God's love, which is "ground," "depth," "ocean." Mother- and nature-symbols are preferred where the relationship to God does not demand obedience but unity, where God is not a distant Other who demands sacrifice and self-denial, but where, instead, agreement and oneness with the Living One are the theme of religion. Solidarity will then replace obedience as the most important virtue.

III. The Father-Symbol

Are there elements in the symbol of God as father that are indispensable for a liberating theology? Does a personal language about God have precedence over other possible symbols? Do we need a "thou" interpreted as "father" to be partner to the human "I"?

In patriarchal culture, the father represents the dependence of the individual. It is biologically given in the fact of being begotten and in the long dependency of the human young, who must be cared for and protected. But does our long childhood justify a religious language essentially oriented to a parent-child relationship? And does not the exclusion of the mother from this relationship, as if it were the father alone who is responsible for conception and survival, emphasize the authoritarian element still more?

The image of the father in Judaism is oriented to the function of the head of the household, who represents a particular legal, religious, pedagogical, and economic authority. He is judge, priest, teacher, and he controls the means of production. Those within this culture who address God as father have experienced these concrete forms of dependence in their own lives, with double intensity if they are women. Only mercy, as the other element in the father-symbol, can make this dependency bearable; the joining of absolute authority with compassion is the mark of the Father-God. Closeness and distance, fatherly kindness and juridical dominion are the poles that determine the image of the father. The history of the Father-God in our culture can be described in terms of the tension between these two poles. But when the concentration of biological and social power roles falls apart and increasingly becomes a thing of the past, is not their religious superelevation also without foundation? What is there in the image of the father that is indispensable?

I think that the central question in every feminist philosophical and theological discussion is about the relationship between dependence and independence. Is independence a liberating word, a central value that women are discovering for themselves, or are there dependencies that cannot be denied? Is it good to make oneself emotionally independent, or does that only get us to where the men are, with their superficial ties that dare not limit the ideologized independence of the male hero? What does it mean anthropologically to be dependent? And what does it mean in society? The field of this internal feminist discussion is also the field of theological decision. Is dependence nothing but a repressive inheritance, or does it belong to our createdness?

We have not made, invented, or located ourselves historically or geographically. The context of our life has a before and after to which we are related and from which we cannot divorce ourselves without injury. We are not alone ontologically. There is—this we must believe—a unity of the world, a wholeness, a goal.

Does not the language about God, the father of the living, express precisely this dependence as solidarity? The text of one of Johann Sebastian Bach's religious songs, taken from Simon Dach (1605–1659), says:

I am, O Lord, within thy might,
tis thou hast brought me to the light,
and you preserve for me my life,
you know the number of my moons,
and when I to this vale of gloom
again must say my last good night.
Where, how and when I am to die,
you know, O Father, more than I.

The "power" of the Lord, who at the end is called "Father," is described here with exactitude: it is begetting, life-creating, life-preserving, and life-ending power. Our being born and our dying are not in our hands. Saying "father" to God means that we do not surrender life and death to vitalistic chance. Seeing the world as creation means to see it as willed, as planned, as good. If speaking of God as father helps us not just to accept our dependence as an earthly lot to be overcome, but to welcome it, accepting our finiteness and creaturehood, then there can be no objection to it. Familial symbols can be liberating if they interpret our dependence theologically, as trust in the father and mother.

Familial symbols for God, speaking of God our Father and God our Mother, can have a liberating character, not because they soften the antihumanist, repressive features of patriarchy, but because they anchor us in nature and in the human family. Then talk of God the Father will no longer be sociologically exploited to strengthen the determination of roles and false dependency; it will not be employed to make us eternal children. Instead, it makes us able to trust in the life that goes beyond our own. It endows us also with confidence in Brother Death.

Notes

1. On what follows, see also my 1968 critique of the Christian ideology of obedience: D. Sölle, *Beyond Mere Obedience*, trans. L. W. Denef (New York: Pilgrim, 1982).

2. Cf. Erich Fromm's fundamental distinction between humanitarian and authoritarian religion in his *Psychoanalysis and Religion* (New Haven, Conn.: Yale University Press, 1950).

3. English trans.: *Christ the Representative: an Essay in Theology after the Death of God*, trans. David Lewis (Philadelphia: Fortress, 1967).

Mary and Martha

THE UNITY OF ACTION AND DREAMS

As I was rereading the story of Mary and Martha, I remembered my childhood. In our Lutheran church in a suburb of Cologne there was a stained-glass window with the legend: "Only one thing is needful!" There sat Mary at Jesus' feet, tender, delicate of limb, humble of mien. Leaning on the table, feet apart, a mixing-bowl in her hand, stood Martha, her other hand lifted in reproach. "Lord, do you not care that my sister has left me to serve alone?" (Luke 10:40). I remember that I could not stand that story.

The Western tradition has seen these two women as prototypes of the contemplative and the active life. But meditation and efficiency, the quiet hearing of the Word and the restless concern for the daily needs of the body, the *vita contemplativa* and the *vita activa*, were not simply contrasted with one another. They were placed in an order of rank derived more from Aristotle than from Jewish thought. The contemplative life was the higher, more spiritual, and more essential; the active, practical life is necessary but inferior. Mary has "chosen the better part" (10:42). Martha is regarded in this tradition as useful but somewhat narrow and restricted. It is one of the basic principles of Western thought to regard "pure" theory as superior to mere practice; they are related to one another as headwork to handwork. It is true that the Reformation suppressed the cloisters of contemplative sisters in favor of practical, bourgeois life, but it further devalued the figure of Martha, the active, realistic woman. Luther said: "Martha, your work must be punished and regarded as worthless. . . . I want no work but that of Mary, which is faith."

It was not the Reformation, but a very different movement that spoke up against the dominance of this spiritualizing and anti-Jewish tradition of interpretation in favor of Mary and against Martha— namely, the mystics. In a radical new interpretation, Meister Eckhart, in his Sermon 28, set the still immature Mary at the beginning of the spiritual life and assigned to the mature Martha, on the basis of her experience, a greater nearness to that which is really necessary. Martha "feared that Mary would remain in this feeling of pleasure and make no further progress." She wants Mary to be like her. Eckhart continues in a brilliant new Christian (not clerical) reading (*relecture*) that reflects the spirit of the growing women's movement of the late Middle Ages: "Then Christ replied to her . . . 'Be reassured, Martha, she has chosen the best part, which will lose itself in her. The highest thing that can happen to a creature will happen to her. She will be as happy as you!' "[1]

Women today who deliberately get involved with the Christian tradition are in the process of learning how to distinguish between the oppressive, woman-hating features of that tradition and the liberating ones. For our story, that means taking two steps. I call the first one "rediscovering Martha," and the second "receiving Mary and Martha together." We not only have to understand Martha, we have to revalue her, accept her strength, make her energy our own. We must see her not with Luke's eyes, but bringing in John 11, the story of the raising of Lazarus. In this story Martha is the actor who strives with Jesus as Job strove with God. She is the realistic, active person who knows that her brother, after four days in the grave, is already putrid, and she is the theological thinker who confesses Christ: "Yes, Lord, I believe that you are the Christ, the Son of God who has come into the world" (11:27)—a profession otherwise spoken only by Peter.

Discovering this Christian woman, as Elisabeth Moltmann-Wendel has done in exemplary fashion,[2] helps us to deflate the hierarchy, even the one that has taken root inside us. Hierarchy as warranted domination that has no need to justify itself, that dispenses superiority and privilege, has always been directed against the deepest interests of women even when, as in the Mary-Martha model, it crops up among women themselves. Hierarchical thinking always undergirds contempt for women, making them comic or trivial. I think I sensed that, even as a little girl. I felt sorry for Martha, and she was an embarrassment. It was painful and distressing that women could be like the Martha cliché I had inherited.

Rediscovering Martha, learning to love the strong, self-confident, sober, clear-headed woman, helps me. In the Lazarus story we also see how differently the two sisters react to the death of their brother. Mary throws herself weeping at Jesus' feet; Martha reproaches him because he was so close by and could have come sooner without any difficulty! She is brash and does not give in. It is she, a female Peter, who speaks the truth. It is no accident that she was later depicted as a dragon-killer.

The other necessary step in interpretation that is of the utmost importance for women *and* men today is also connected to the re-discovery of this Martha who had been made so ugly for us. We have to learn that we need not choose between contemplation and action. No one has the right to compel us to this choice. We need not divide the world into doers and dreamers, into gentle, listening, self-surrendering Marys on the one side and pragmatic, busy Marthas on the other. We need both Mary and Martha, for in fact we ourselves are both sisters. Teresa of Avila, who followed the mystical tradition of interpretation and condemned a contemplation that is closed in on itself, said: "Believe me, Martha and Mary must be together in order to give lodging to the Lord and have him always with them. Otherwise he would be badly served and remain unfed. How could Mary, who was always sitting at his feet, have given him anything to eat if her sister had not come to help her? But his food is that we gather souls in every possible way, so that they may be saved and may praise him forever."[3] It is only the two sisters together who can "give lodging to" Christ so that he has a place in the world.

Nowadays in the rich world there is a great longing for spirituality, for immersion, for contemplation and mysticism. Mary can symbolize this half-developed, still immature spirituality. Many young people despair of the possibilities of action in our world; they see the trees dying and the children of the poor starving, and they retreat into an inwardness about which the mystics warned us. Eckhart says of Mary that at that time, while she was sitting at the feet of Christ, "she was still not the true Mary. . . . For she sat still in a feeling of pleasure and sweetness, was received into the school, and learned how to live. But Martha remained quite real there."[4]

I always think of this distinction when I see the strong women of my generation who act unflinchingly and struggle against the dragon that controls us. They have broken openly and unequivocally with the racists in South Africa; they stand in front of the big stores and they talk with the people in the little shops on the corner; they call on the bank directors; they say loudly and unambiguously what they think. In these groups of women who for years have been organizing the boycott, "Don't buy the fruits of apartheid," I see a lot of Marthas together, just as in the women who put a girdle around the other big dragon who lives in the Pentagon and began to act against it. That is the Martha whom Meister Eckhart saw, the one the people of southern France pictured as a dragon-slayer, who, according to a folk legend, crossed the sea with her sister Mary in order to teach and to preach. If one day our churches would "give lodging to" Christ and feed him, such women would be the bishops and teachers of the church. The Martha in me ought not to repress the Mary. In every woman, the young girl she once was should be visible. But the best women I know are no longer willing to accept the either-or.

When I was a little girl, the youngest after three brothers, I sometimes had to hide my Indian books and pretend to be doing my homework in order to escape the "snares of mediocrity," as Kierkegaard so exactly described it. Most women know the problem of having to make a place for themselves where they have the freedom to grow and not to be kept artificially small. It is clear that Mary and Martha in the Bible also express a mother-daughter problem. But the Bible transforms mothers and daughters into sisters, and the legend allows them both to cross the sea with Jesus' disciples and to teach and preach, so that they have both action and dreams, doing justice and praying, *lutte et contemplation*, in their lives—and the world becomes a more sisterly place.

Notes

1. Meister Eckhart, *Deutsche Predigten und Traktate* (Munich: C. Hanser, 1955), 286. English trans. in Fox, *Breakthrough*, 480–84.

2. Elisabeth Moltmann-Wendel, *The Women Around Jesus* (New York: Crossroad, 1982).

3. J. Sudbrack, *Erfahrung einer Liebe, Teresa von Avilas Mystik als Begegnung mit Gott* (Freiburg: Herder, 1979).

4. Fox, *Breakthrough*, 485.

God, Mother
of Us All

"May God bless and protect you. May she let her face shine upon you and be gracious to you." These words of blessing at the end of a worship service in St. Catharine's Church in Hamburg were very differently received by different people. For many, they represented a great liberation, while others felt themselves alienated, some of them even threatened.

If it is true, as Meister Eckhart said, that we have "driven out images through images," then at the present time we can point to a moment in the history of religion where this is happening consistently and creatively: in feminist theology. Women today are beginning to name God, not in the language of the fathers or of the sons, but in their own language. They no longer need a tutor to teach them the names and images for God, because they are beginning to speak for themselves.

God is still most often addressed as male. The numerical surplus of divine attributes with male gender is shocking. In the ecumenical movement and in many places in the United States this kind of sexist language is regarded as inappropriate, even insulting. Pope John Paul I explained in 1978 that God is at least as much mother as father. Shouldn't this relationship of "at least as much" somehow express itself theologically? It is high time we demanded a little more progress in transcending the existing, established language in the direction of something new.

Patriarchy's God-talk falls short of divine transcendence. A God who can only be called "he" is too small. The divine must be described in the categories of a harmonious but dynamic relation of contraries: omnipresent and hidden, omnipotent and powerless, mother and father. Allah has ninety-nine names, which means that *one* name for God is not sufficient—in fact, it leads to error! Wanting to name God with a single word is an attempt to control God and to put God at our disposition. Therefore God refuses Moses' demand for a name by which to know God and says: "I will be he who I will be" (Exod. 3:14). Better still, because it expresses the element of freedom and uncontrollability, I now translate this Hebrew sentence as: "I will be she who I will be."

God surpasses God, as the process theologians say. Like every good theological statement, this also has a critical, exclusive sense that implies that a God who does not surpass God is no God. God, trapped in a particular language, delimited by particular definitions, known by names that have been established by particular sociocultural forms of domination, is not God but a religious ideology. Symbols like that of the omnipotence of God tell me more about the projections and desires of the men who use them than about God. Names can become prisons for God.

"Therefore I pray God," says Meister Eckhart, "that he rid me of God." That is no heresy. It is a prayer for liberation from the prison of a language that is too small for God. I would understand Eckhart today as saying: therefore I pray God my mother that she rid me of the male God.

A symbol that is no longer understood as a symbol, but as the thing itself, is a prison. I had an existential experience of that when I prayed the Our Father for the first time in its ecumenical form: "Our Father and Mother in heaven, hallowed be thy name . . ." It was like the moment when someone opens the windows in a vacation cottage: light entered, air streamed in, the long winter was at an end. It was not so much the new name for God (Our Mother) that empowered me as the consciousness of having crossed a line, of having left a prison. "Father" alone, I felt, is a dead word. "Father and Mother" is an invitation to go in search of more names for God. God became more sayable. "Our Father and Mother" opened out toward sister, friend, compañera. . . . My fantasies that had been fettered by patriarchy were set free.

As lovers are never tired of inventing new names for one another, so it is also in the relationship with Love itself, with God. In a living relationship the name does not pertain to a thing, as the word *table* refers to a particular function. When old formulas die, we become aware of the defunct relationship that is still administered by religious functionaries, and whose name is so well established that it no longer needs any other name. In this sense one can say that God dies by the habit of calling "him" God.

"In the name of God, our Father and Mother; in the name of Jesus, our brother and savior; and in the name of the Holy Spirit, he who comforts us and she who gives us courage!" In this liturgical formula, with which a pastor and friend of mine opens every Sunday service, the "name" has taken on a new meaning. It is a liberating and not a commanding element. It does not simply cover a known thing with a name, but it does what all living language does: it invites us to communicate more, to share more, to go beyond the limits of what has already been said. A name calls to the other, and every new name of God calls forth other and more names. In this sense the divine name "Mother of us all" is not supposed to replace the name of father, as men often fear; but it relativizes it, and that is necessary in order to call attention to the fundamental lie of patriarchy, which consists of defining the human being as "man," with the consequence that all language about God remains equally androcentric.

In contrast to other religious traditions of East and West, it is a characteristic of the three monotheistic religions (Judaism, Christianity, and Islam) that they lack feminine symbols for God. The God of Israel did not share his power with any female divinity—differing thus from many contemporary religious traditions in the Near East. Nor was YHWH the husband or lover of any goddess. The biblical symbols for him are sometimes masculine: he is king, Lord, master, judge, and father. And yet we read in Isaiah: "As one whom his mother comforts, so will I comfort you" (66:13). Images of God, who "will not break a bruised reed" (Isa. 42:3), or of a sparrow, who "has found a home, and the swallow a nest for herself, where she may lay her young, at thy altars . . ." (Psalms 84) point toward another, non-androcentric language, in the Bible also.

There is a song in the American women's movement about a little girl. It says: "May the warm wind caress you, may God smile, may she bless you." God smiles, she blesses, she comforts. Warmth, softness, tenderness, safety, richness of emotion—all these are characteristics of God, even if in our culture they are projected onto women, delegated to them and thereby degraded. In public discussions I am often sneered at by men for being "emotional." It sounds to me as if such men are proud of their own emotional underdevelopment. I always experience that as a sign of distorted religiosity. Perhaps such men have never met God our mother, God our sister.

It was not always that way. There are sources from early Christianity, from the first two centuries, that unite masculine and feminine elements in God. The teacher and poet Valentinian images the divine as dual, existing partly as the "unutterable," the "depth," the "original father," and partly as "grace," "silence," the "mother-womb," and the "mother of the universe."

These Gnostic traditions and texts were later declared heretical and denounced. During the first twenty years after Jesus' death, individual women had leading positions in the communities and held office as prophets, healers, teachers, and evangelists. In the Gnostic Christian sects of Marcionites, Valentinians, Carpocratians, and Montanists there were even women bishops. This "woman-loving feminism" disappears from the early church at the beginning of the third century, in both its elements: the feminine features in the God-image and the active participation of women in community leadership. Orthodoxy sanctioned the divinely willed rule of the man over the woman. Tertullian, for example, was repelled by "insolent and presumptuous heretical women." God the father won out over God the mother then. Of the hundred names of God, only fifty are allowed to be spoken.

There is a division in the religious women's movement today because of the destructive woman-hating tradition of Christianity. On the one hand we find the "post-Christian" spirituality of women who often draw their names for God from other religions and place at the center of their worship the great Demeter, Mother Earth, Gaia, or other symbols of warmth, wholeness, and fertility. They can no longer express their experience of God in Jewish-Christian terms. Others, I among them, understand Christianity as a doctrine of liberation that also frees us from the domination of men over women. We believe that God, even the Jewish-Christian God, is more than can be grasped in masculine images. We think that the liberating elements in the tradition we have received are stronger even than the subtle idolatry practiced at the altar of patriarchy. We are trying to speak differently and in new ways about God without denying or destroying ourselves or conforming ourselves to the men. We are seeking to overcome the fear of femaleness that emerges in so many of the names of God that deny God's womanly side—to overcome them in ourselves and to make that process an inviting one also for men, who, in the culture of male dominance, can only articulate their own humanity in ways that are mutilating and self-destructive.

Here is an example drawn from the history of this emerging spirituality: Not long ago I was in a group working on the topic of piety and feminism. We had gotten to the nadir, so it appeared. Linguistic confusion, political differences, and emotional conflicts seemed very hard to overcome. Some talked, others withdrew into silence, and the Holy Spirit, the *Ruach,* who consoles us and leads us to truth, was not there. One woman suggested that we stand up, make a circle, and hold one another's hands. Each would then speak a name for God. As each of us, in this ritual, said what we wanted to call the ground of our life, we came close to each other again. I remember some of these names for God:

> Living Water
> Sister
> The one who gives me courage
> The shining eyes of my baby son
> Father and Mother of us all
> Everything is possible
> Fire

This ritual helped us. I think that the names of God must be shared in order to be names. We have to say them to one another. If God is, as Meister Eckhart said, "total communication," the power of being-in-relationship, then we are united with God at that moment when we share God. Giving names is a form of communicating, and what we are trying to do is to communicate God. Name calls to name.

PART THREE
Cells of Resistance

The Three
Theologies

When I was studying theology at Göttingen in the fifties there were—
apart from the fundamentalists, whom nobody took seriously—two
relevant positions, represented by Karl Barth and Rudolf Bultmann.
At the beginning of the sixties, especially in the wake of the student
movement, these two positions and their controversies faded into the
background. There followed a long period in which the theological
landscape was obscure: no mountains stood out plainly, there were
no works that caused schools to form, no controversies that went to
the root of things, or at least that is how it appeared. Instead, there
were rediscoveries, cautious approaches to empirical reality. Developments were made in connection with the human and social sciences: psychology, sociology, social psychology, and psychoanalysis.
The thesis of the secularization of Christian faith, so celebrated at the
time, seemed to be corroborated within the theological discipline itself.

At the beginning of the eighties this diffuse situation changed. There
are now three discernible theological tendencies, which I will call,
respectively, conservative, liberal, and radical. I could as easily call
them orthodox, liberal, and liberation theologies. In considering all
these "file drawers" or categories, it is important to keep in mind the
connection between the theological and the political. The three theologies are basic theological-political models that apply to both those
realms, theology and politics. They are not fundamental theological
convictions that could then find a political application as well, though
they would not need to do so. Nor are they, as the conservatives like

to say, political options that deck themselves out in a few theological garments. Instead, there are basic theological decisions behind the political conflicts. Tell me how you think and act politically, and I will tell you who your God is.

An anecdote from the sixties will illustrate this. A pastor who worked in industry was interviewed on television about worker participation. He said, standing before the factory entrance: "There ought to be a sign here saying, 'You are now leaving the democratic sector.' " The next day he was called in by his superintendent and told that an objection had been received from the highest level. "From the highest level? Do you mean God? or the bishop?" he asked. Answer: "No, the board of directors."

The disagreement among the three positions really is theological-political. Every serious theological proposition has a political point directed at the state of the world. The statement that "the earth is the Lord's" (Ps. 24:1) disputes the ruling power of the directors of multinationals. In the death of Jesus, however it may be theologically interpreted or spiritualized, Pontius Pilate and the power of the state are always present.

I have debated with myself whether I ought to speak of only two current theologies, which I would then have to call theology of liberation and theology of the bourgeoisie; or whether I should use more nuance and include in the picture the two very different developments of bourgeois theology in the conservative and liberal camps. In the framework of a biblical discussion for the Church Congress at Düsseldorf in 1985 I used the reduced model and described the two principal theologies of today as two confessions that can no longer be categorized within the confessions of the sixteenth century, when Christians defined themselves as Catholic or Protestant. For the readers of this book, however, the more differentiated analysis seems to me more useful; I am addressing myself to readers who are confronted in their daily lives with both types of bourgeois theology and who often may even be rubbed raw by their conflicts, though they themselves hope to see bourgeois theology overcome by liberation theology.

I. Neoconservative Civic Religion

Conservative or orthodox theology takes the Bible and dogmatic tradition as its starting point. Faith means believing acceptance of the truth revealed in the tradition; or, in the words of the first thesis of the Barmen Theological Declaration of 1954: "Jesus Christ, as witnessed for us in the Holy Scriptures, is the one Word of God whom we are to hear, to trust in life and in death, and to obey." These are the words of a theology from above, anchored in conservatism and stamped by Karl Barth's neoorthodoxy. People are made subject to "revelation," they are to "hear," "trust," and "obey." Other "events and powers, beings and truths," as we read in the explanatory repudiation attached to this thesis, *cannot* be recognized as revelation. In the context of the struggle with Nazism and its German Christian adherents it was obvious which "truths" (for example, the superiority of the Aryan race), what "other powers" (such as Blood and Soil), and what "beings" (namely Adolf Hitler, the Führer) were meant here.

But outside this historical situation the thesis is theologically ambiguous. Orthodoxy does not reflect on its own cultural prejudices; instead, it transfigures them. It does not think in terms of the sociology of knowledge and has no suspicions about its own ideology. It carries on its reflection without a context, and consequently it is possible that the thesis once directed against the German Christians may be interpreted today in neoorthodox and conservative terms something like this:

Jesus Christ is above all worldly systems. Taking his side means refusing to get involved in the struggles of this world. Every kind of political engagement on the part of the church is to be condemned; being a Christian sets one definitively at a distance from any sort of practical engagement in political questions. Christ transcends culture and history. He is a changeless, autonomous divine being beyond all our hopes and visions—which, accordingly, are to be regarded as purely ideological opinions, all of them equally far from the one Word of God.

The lack of context in this orthodox and neoorthodox theology is dangerous, and this includes its fetishism about words. By this I mean its inability to recognize what was originally meant in the Bible when it is given different expression. There is a certain kind of inflexibility, fettered by tradition, that reifies certain concepts such as Christ, salvation, and justification by faith alone, as if they no longer needed to become flesh; as if their mere recitation enunciated the faith with all the clarity necessary. Spiritual rigidity and an addiction to the repetition of what has been clearly stated in the past are characteristic of this bent. If a New Testament concept such as *agape* is now translated as "solidarity," because the traditional rendition with "love" does not transmit the content of the word clearly enough, theological conservatives become anxious, for theological-political reasons.

Biblicism is literalist and clings to the letter of the written word in the context of a particular cultural situation in the lower middle class, which sees itself threatened by economic and social decline, isolation, and dissolution of its traditional values—those of sexual morality, for example. Conservative theology reacts to this threat with word-fetishist repetition that more often silently presumes (instead of naming) the ideological content (such as parental rule over the young; compulsory assignment of roles to women; distance and hostility toward all forms of political expression, from letters of protest to silent vigils). Sin is localized in the heart of the individual and not in economic structures. Peace is to be realized in the family and in the upbringing of children. Everything outside the narrowest circle of individual and family life already belongs to "politicization" of faith and is rejected. The idea that individualization itself is the most dangerous ideologizing of faith is to be firmly denied.

And yet the conservative position today is not confined to defining, rejecting, and drawing limits. At least in the United States the religious Right has become newly aware of its economic and political power. Since the beginning of the eighties the religious Right in the United States has discovered a new offensive political role through its alliance with the extreme political Right. Whereas at an earlier period, in the Pietist era of the eighteenth century, devout fundamentalists were known as the "silent ones in the country," today their piety has become earsplitting, demanding, publicly visible, and voicing claims to authority.

The previous American president, under the pressure of these groups whose ultraconservative capital helped him gain power in 1980, propagated the neoconservative ideology and religion more and more visibly. In his speech to the National Association of Evangelicals, Ronald Reagan said: "I do believe that HE has begun to heal our blessed land." He meant by this not only economic growth as a reward for the true faithful (a popular form of the Max Weber thesis!), but also the "spiritual reawakening" of America. He said in Columbus, Ohio: "Americans are turning back to God. Church attendance is up. Audiences for religious books and broadcasts are growing." This process of healing, according to Reagan, began with his presidency. The time before it was gloomy and lost. America, said Reagan, "did seem to lose her religious and moral bearings—to forget the faith and values that made us good and great." "But the Almighty [a word Hitler used more and more often in the last years, after Stalingrad] who gave us this great land, also gave us free will—the power under God to choose our own destiny. The American people decided to put a stop to that long decline, and today our country is seeing a rebirth of freedom and faith—a great national renewal."[1]

George Gilder produced an economic primer for the neoconservatives, entitled *Wealth and Poverty*,[2] which expressly concluded that a particular faith was required to stabilize the system: the belief that it was good to work hard and invest, and that it was necessary to keep women and other troublemakers under control. As symptoms of America's moral decline Reagan mentions pornography, drug addiction, and the collapse of the family, which once was "the cornerstone of our society." His view of history is as follows: "All our material wealth and all our influence is based on our faith in God and the basic values that follow from that belief."

What are these values that form the new civic religion? They are the traditional ones: nation, work, and family. In this context I recall a historical parallel drawn from the period of German occupation of France. Between 1940 and 1944, France had to mint new coins that no longer bore the motto *liberté, égalité, fraternité* (liberty, equality, brotherhood), but substituted the conservative trio *patrie, travail, famille* (fatherland, work, family).

Those are the religious values of neoconservatism. "America is great because America is good," as President Reagan said to the evangelical leaders. The country of these good and just people, which guarantees world peace, must be made strong by means of the greatest collection of armaments in history. Americans are encouraged to believe in the moral superiority of the United States, and the organs of Christian religion are made instruments of this purpose.

The military-political doctrine of national security has replaced the older political values and convictions of democracy, freedom of the press, and human rights; instead, "national security" has become the foundation of policy. A threat to national security is the greatest risk, and its betrayal is a capital crime. We have to keep in mind that the disappearance of human beings, torture, and murder in Latin America and in other Third World countries are ordered and justified in the name of national security. The concept of national security is smeared with the blood of a hundred thousand victims. The crimes of the police and of governments of terror, and the crime of the so-called democracies, namely, arming themselves and others to death, are committed in the name of national security. The quest for national security is part of the new conservative ideology with its rhetoric of strength, its threats (open or concealed) to those who think differently, its reduction of every conflict in the world to the East-West struggle, and so on.

The program has a military exterior, but at the same time it has a religious and cultural interior. The fundamentalist movement, massively funded by the extreme Right, belongs in this context. This movement has also annexed to itself the traditional conservatives who understand themselves as "nonpolitical." Thus the Christocentrism of neoorthodoxy serves as an effective tool against the liberation theology groups who oppose racism and sexism as sin. God's peace is distanced to the greatest extent possible from the question of further acquisition of armaments, and the doctrine of justification "by faith alone" is not supposed to have anything to do with the real ideology of security, nuclear deterrence, where we in fact put our trust in life and death. Denial of reality and repression of one's own part in its construction are necessary preliminaries if the house of neoconservative civil religion is to be built up. Orthodox theology (with its Christocentrism, its distance from the world, its confusion of sin and powerlessness, its anthropological pessimism, its sexism) takes care of this preliminary work, even if it does not engage in the construction of the ideological house itself.

In developed neoconservative civil religion, hard work is enthroned next to national security as the highest value. There is no sympathy for those who do not work. In the context of Reaganomics this meant, in politico-economic terms: no health care for the mass of the old, the sick, and the so-called unemployable; no more food stamps because—as Edwin Meese, Reagan's White House aide, opined, there is no hunger in the United States, not even when people are buying cat food in order to have a little protein. The denial of reality, the refusal to acknowledge certain things that do not accord with the ideology, is in my opinion characteristic of aggressive neoconservatism and differs from older forms of conservatism that still maintained a certain sense of reality, however restricted. In West Germany, for example, the demands of Heiner Geissler, the general secretary of the Christian Democratic party, that a distinction be drawn between good unemployed people and bad people unwilling to work represents a step in the same direction.

The third value in neoconservative civic religion is the family and, within it, the woman's role. Being religious means keeping women in their God-given place. It is not the atomic bomb that threatens our survival! No, love between two men or two women endangers everything we have achieved! The moral scandal of our times is not the starvation of millions of children in the Third World as a result of our masterful economic planning, but the destruction of unborn life! Unemployment is not the problem, pornography is! Neoconservatism and the new civic religion promise security through nationalism, work, and family. It is a vision for the haves, not for the have-nots. It will ensure that we keep what we have.

2. Helpless Liberalism

Liberal theology is disgusted by the recent rapprochement between orthodox fundamentalist Christianity and national might. It is marked by the critical spirit of the Enlightenment: biblical criticism, critique of domination and of institutions are indispensable to it. Therefore liberal theology approves the separation of church and state as a fundamental principle. And in fact it was absolutely necessary for an economic and sociopolitical system that functions according to the principles of the free market economy to distance itself from the moral, religious, and transcendent dimensions of human existence.

At an early stage of liberalism, the rising middle class was the bearer of an enlightened vision of an autonomous society that would no longer be ruled by the church or by the strange alliance of nobility and clergy. It was in the interest of the liberal state to protect itself from a church that was regarded as power-hungry; it wanted to let the church be church, at a safe distance from the world of politics.

Today, as we approach the end of the liberal epoch (a phenomenon especially noticeable in the United States at the present time), it is just the other way around: the church, as a middle-class institution, has an interest in keeping itself apart from the political and economic decisions of the modern state. Official Protestantism, which we have to regard as a middle-class religion, has retreated to the moral and transcendent aspects of Christian faith; it has silenced its socioeconomic demands for the whole of human life and society.

During the French Revolution and the beginnings of Jeffersonian democracy it was the state that desired and needed freedom from unenlightened and unscientific clericalism. The church, in its middle-class Protestant form, accommodated itself to the demands of modernity, the Enlightenment, and the sciences. But in the process the church lost its critical and prophetic voice, because it recognized the division of life into two worlds, one devoted to economics and politics and the other private, with religious matters confined to the latter. Each world had a certain autonomous identity; taken together they represented the historical reality of the bourgeois era.

But this prestabilized harmony was deceptive. It yielded nothing for the human rights of racial minorities like the Jews in Europe or blacks in the United States. It did nothing for the poor; neither for the landless peasants nor for the industrial proletariat did the separation of church and state function positively to achieve emancipation, nor even conservatively to protect them—to say nothing of the marginalized masses we find in the Third World today. The bourgeois liberal ideology insisted that the secular and sacred dimensions of the modern world had created a historical situation in which the state took care of economics and politics, while the church protected and saved the souls of private persons. But this liberal myth never really functioned for the oppressed. As state oppression took new forms in the twentieth century, such as concentration camps, and as torture became a normal means of interrogation, the myth of separation of church and state collapsed, and at least some parts of Christianity rediscovered their own visionary demand to change not only private individuals, but the machinery of society as well.

The collapse of liberalism, brought on by twentieth-century Fascism, challenged and polarized the church—in Nazi Germany, in Franco's Spain, and today in South Africa and Latin America. The beautiful harmony of separation of church and state could not survive in the face of the growth of totalitarianism in the state. And the church, under Hitler, Franco, Pinochet, Somoza, and (increasingly) the CIA, saw itself challenged by violations of human rights. A political apparatus that demands absolute obedience and total submission to its ideology forces the church at the present time to review its own liberal history; the political debate in the United States, in my own observation, is being increasingly theologized.

We are living at a time when two religions, the religion of the state and the religion of resistance, are struggling with one another. This means the end of the liberal era and specifically the falsification of its thesis about the secularization of society. History has refuted those who thought that religion would die of itself, that it was irrelevant for politics and individual decision, and that the Enlightenment, as one favorite tenet of intellectuals held, would ultimately make religion obsolete. In this sense the presuppositions of the liberal era are no longer valid. We have to ask whether a theology can maintain its integrity within an amicable separation of church and state. It could not do so in 1933; liberalism was more or less a failure in that situation, just as liberal theology had failed in 1914 (to Karl Barth's disgust!) at the outbreak of World War I. Today theology is under heavy pressure to restrict itself to individual souls. The church is to make the meaning of life clear to the unemployed; under no circumstances should it ask questions about the causes of unemployment.

The second key point about liberal theology is its individualism, by which one may most easily recognize it. It regards the human person as a separate being that finds comfort and peace of soul in believing. Modern life treats us all harshly enough—stress, competition, and human loneliness are enormous—and it is precisely in this area that the Christian religion ought to offer us consolation and healing as our salvation from evil. In this perspective, the kingdom of God is totally suppressed in favor of individual salvation. "Deliver us from evil" is more important than "Thy kingdom come," although in reality the two petitions belong together. Bourgeois theology is the work of the androcentrically thinking middle class: white, relatively well-to-do, shaped and determined by men. It disregards the suffering masses of the earth; the starving appear, if at all, as objects of charity. Otherwise, problems of sexual ethics or of death and dying are much more important for this theology than are social, political, or economic questions.

3. *Theology of Liberation*

Besides these two theologies there has been, for about twenty years now, a theology that is not done by white, relatively well-to-do males: the theology of liberation. In this theology, faith is not experienced first of all as a consolation for an ordinary and often wretched life, but as a way of living, hoping, and acting. It means a revolution in human hearts corresponding to the words of Jesus to a man who had been lame for many years: "Get up! Take up your bed and walk!" (Mark 2:9) Christ doesn't just console, he changes our lives. Just as for Jesus' first disciples—poor and ignorant people, the majority of whom were women—in the communities of faith springing up at the base, we see emerging a way of living and sharing with one another, of organizing, celebrating, and struggling together. In a great many cases this new kind of life causes the Christians to be despised and avoided, to be barred from many occupations; in the Third World, persecution, torture, and death for the faith are more and more common.

Liberation theology is happening among the poor, in the South African townships, in the refugee camps in El Salvador, among the women textile workers in Sri Lanka. But that in no way means that it is unimportant for us here. We are, after all, not without our share in the misery that is the lot of people in two-thirds of the world today: we are part of the problem. Our country's representatives at international conferences, those sponsored by the United Nations, for example, usually vote with the representatives of the USA against all proposals made by the poor countries for the sake of changing the politico-economic situation. We are not spectators, we are not victims—we are the culprits who cause the misery. Therefore theology of liberation is not some kind of fashionable theology that we can take or leave alone. It is God's gift to us today, an expression of the faith of people in the First World as well, those who live for the sake of liberation from the terrible role of those who plunge the innocent into misery, condemn children to death, and repress the hopes of the poor through police states, military dictatorships, and open warfare.

Liberation theology, too, orients itself to the one Word of God, Jesus Christ. But it does not leave this Word to stand without a context, as if it were suprahistorical or addressed to the depth of the individual soul. The one Word of God in the understanding of liberation theology is the messianic praxis of Jesus and his followers. Christ is not the one Word of God because he is formally superior to all other ideological or religious demands, or because he, in contrast to all others, speaks of God. The foundation of faith is not that it was Christ who spoke with divine authority; the foundation of faith is the praxis of this poor man from Nazareth who shared his bread with the hungry and made the blind see, and who lived and died for justice. Listening to authority does not get us anywhere, but praxis does. It is a basic principle of liberation theology that the poor are the teachers. So we are learning today mainly from and through the poor: not technology, not facts, but faith and hope.

Recently a young Swiss teacher asked me, in the course of a conversation about the situation of the peoples oppressed by Western nations, where I found any reason to hope. At first I wanted to say to him: "From my faith in God, who has already rescued an oppressed people once before from slavery to a powerful military state!" But then it occurred to me that it is really not "my" faith that supports me. It is the faith and hope of the poor who do not give up. As long as they do not despair and surrender, as long as they go on, we haven't the least right to whine, to speak resignedly out of our analysis that counts money and weapons but does not reckon with the pride of the oppressed and their willingness to struggle, and to say there is nothing we can do!

Radical theology goes to the roots of our fear of powerlessness and assures us that "all things are possible," as it says in one of the liberating stories in the New Testament.

4. Distinguishing God from the Idols

This description of the present theological situation would be incomplete without the practical-missionary dimension. How do people get from one camp to the other? We have to look for connections, passages, conversions. Christian Beyers-Naudé, for example, was a conservative South African theologian from an old Boer family who, at the age of fifty, became a liberation theologian fighting against apartheid. Are there rebellious traits within orthodox theology that can prevent its being incorporated in Western anticommunist ideology? Where are the bridges between critical left-liberal positions and the praxis of liberation? What parts of these differing positions do we find in ourselves?

One sign of false religion is that in it, God and Satan are indistinguishable. That applies also to the fundamentalists who predict the end of the world as God's will and work toward it with their politics. God, for them, is neither love nor justice, but sheer power. The militarization of the whole world is the accomplishment of this God; strength is his highest ideal, violence his method, security his promise.

The movement for more peace and justice that is producing a kind of liberation theology among us has freed itself from this God. This liberation means turning away from false life and turning toward another form of life.

What is at stake is a lifelong conversion.

Literature

Franz J. Hinkelammert, *The Ideological Weapons of Death: A Theological Critique of Capitalism.* Translated by Philip Berryman (Maryknoll, N.Y.: Orbis, 1985).

Ruben Alves, *Protestantism and Repression. A Brazilian Case Study* (Maryknoll, N.Y.: Orbis, 1985).

D. Sölle and L. Schottroff, *Die Erde gehört Gott. Texte zur Bibelarbeit von Frauen* (Reinbek: Rowohlt, 1985).

Notes

1. *New York Times*, 7 March 1984.
2. George Gilder, *Wealth and Poverty* (New York: Basic Books, 1981).

Søren Kierkegaard and the Concept of Anxiety

I was twenty years old when I discovered Søren Kierkegaard. I was mired in one of those deep crises of meaning and identity that afflict young people in our culture. It was 1949, and one of the philosophical conclusions drawn by my generation from recent events in Europe was existential nihilism. Sartre, Camus, and Heidegger described where we were. Kierkegaard was counted the father of these fathers, but I knew, after the first twenty pages, that he had something— hidden? withdrawn? only indirectly communicated?—that the fathers had not handed on to us: radical religion; transcendence of the factual situation; passion for the unconditional. I read in Kierkegaard about the five foolish virgins in the gospel who had the door shut in their faces because they had no oil, that they had become "unrecognizable in the spiritual sense because they had lost the eternal passion."

Kierkegaard seduced me into religion. I devoured him. Today I could say that I fell in love with Søren. Is there really any better way to learn something? At that time I would have rejected this expression as inappropriate. But my fantasies as I read, my intensive dialogue with Søren over a period of months, tended in a quite unscholarly direction: If I had been Regine . . . why was it necessary to break the engagement . . . what does sexuality mean when someone has found "his category" . . . why does Søren, who is certainly not brutal or trivial, say these insulting things about women? . . . I submerged myself in Kierkegaard.

Each time I read him again I was fascinated by the apparent arrogance and inner humility of his style. Is it not partly arrogance, that "permissible self-defense and one especially pleasing to God, against the snares of the mediocre" to make anxiety, in the Copenhagen of 1844, a central theme? To assert that animals and angels can live without anxiety, but not the human being, that spiritual being that has a relationship with itself? "In spiritlessness there is no anxiety because it is too happy, too content, and too spiritless for that."[1] I read this sentence today existentially by applying it to my own religious-political situation and thinking of the NATO leaders, ministers of defense, and politicians who direct my life.

Anxiety, according to Kierkegaard, is a moment that changes us, that drives us to conversion. Always opposed to rashness, superficiality, and rationalism, Kierkegaard as a writer tries to speak "seriously," to communicate himself "existentially." "Seriousness and temperament correspond to one another in such a way that seriousness is a higher and also the deepest expression of that which temperament is. Temperament is a determination of immediacy and therefore is, literarily speaking, helpless. The seriousness of the writer is the originality of temperament achieved through the process of reflection." It is thus the duty of the one who writes (how much more so if the writer is a woman!) not to ignore or suppress temperament, but to purify it so that it becomes seriousness. In literary terms, this seriousness consists of saying nothing superfluous or trivial, of repudiating redundancy in thought, while at the same time searching for it in temperament. What is unbearable in thought, and destructive of seriousness, is repetition, redundancy. Feeling, however, requires repetition, it demands time. If a kiss were a bit of information, one would be enough, and all others would be redundant and verbose. But a kiss is an existential communication.

Kierkegaard was neither a poet nor a philosopher; he was a preacher in a secularized society who explained and defended Christian faith—as absurd an undertaking for a Christianity co-opted by bourgeois society as for the efficient, business-minded world.

He distinguishes three stages of existence: the aesthetic, the ethical, and the religious forms of life. "The concept of anxiety" has its locus precisely at the point of transition from the ethical to the religious stage. Those who are spiritless enough not to be afraid can settle down in the ethical stage and live in a kind of social democratic reductionism. A radical ethic, on the other hand, becomes religious; it "founders" on sins by means of repentance.[2] The radical ethic exposes itself to anxiety, to loss of life, "to remaining in death" as John's first letter says, "to being bereft of category." Anxiety is the dialectically understood strength of attraction and repulsion, as we sense in the double meaning of words like *fearful* and *anxious*. Anxiety flees before guilt; it wants to remain innocent and at the same time it is drawn into guilt.

In contrast to fear, anxiety is not directed to individual, determinable objects. It is a basic human emotion that arises out of the totality of one's being. It can, to be sure, blend with our attitudes to various objects, but it contains an existential core that is difficult to deny. Ontological anxiety (which Freud would call neurotic) is opposed to simple ontic fear. Anxiety in this sense has to do with nothing; it is through the mediation of anxiety that we encounter nothingness. In anxiety, nothingness reaches out for us.

But Kierkegaard did not elevate this nothingness to an ideological nihilism; he did not proceed from the *nihil* of anxiety to nihilism, but to a faith that was later described by Tillich as "the courage to be." Courage presupposes anxiety and the overcoming of anxiety. Kierkegaard the preacher thus regarded anxiety, which attacks us when we face up to the limitlessness of possibility, as an uplifting and redeeming power that draws us to God as it drives us out of our spiritless, peaceful snugness. In anxiety we are driven to our limits, to the point where we dare the leap of faith—which is a leap into precisely that nothingness of anxiety. Those who leap into their own anxiety do not and cannot know whether God will catch them or whether the nothingness will devour them. Kierkegaard says that the believer is swimming above a depth of 70,000 fathoms. This negative infinity is the Highest; how is the swimmer to know whether she or he has solid ground below?

Vigilius Haufniensis, the Watchman of Copenhagen, Kierkegaard's pseudonym in writing this, did not make it easy for us. His phenomenological view of anxiety, its rediscovery, is more obscured than otherwise by the dogma of original sin and by his sexual psychology, which, with all affection for Søren, must be described as gloomy. Nevertheless we may perceive a structure of the "concept of anxiety" developed in four theological steps:

1. The greatness of the human being depends solely on the energy of the relationship to God. We want to know and love God, which means to become love itself.

2. The more deeply we desire this, the more clearly we recognize *guilt*, our separation from God, our inability to become love totally.

3. Between fully self-chosen existence and guilt stands *anxiety*, which we can only avoid if we become spiritless and unfree. "The relation is freedom's possibility."[3]

4. Anxiety is simply the constructive power of faith, insofar as it destroys all that is finite and uncovers all deceptions.[4] It is not spiritlessness, but anxiety that leads to *faith*, in which we renounce anxiety.

This path from guilt by way of anxiety to faith is a way of freedom; it is an attempt to enunciate anew the oldest themes of Western theology about the "happy fault."

If we regard ourselves as unfree—and that is normal for pagans—the relationship of necessity (called "force of circumstances" in political jargon) to guilt is fate. We will skid fatalistically into the Third World War. The fatalism of the pressures of circumstance has to repress anxiety, which is a creative moment of change, and it does not require a great deal of fantasy even today to imagine a national power that would criminalize all those who are still capable of anxiety.

For Kierkegaard, anxiety is on the side of freedom, not on that of necessity. But we are totally free only when we "renounce anxiety without anxiety," that is, when we believe. In anxiety we seek and flee our guilt; in faith we acknowledge it. In anxiety we permit ourselves to be fascinated and terrified by the nothingness of our own weakness; in faith we admit our powerlessness and become empty for the power of God that appears in the solidarity of the weak. The last chapter is called "Anxiety as saving through faith." Anxiety is a precondition of faith; those who are spiritless and without anxiety cannot believe, because nothing compels them to it. They stick with their bombs and file cards.

What is at stake is a passion for the infinite, for that which surpasses all the possibilities I can now recognize. Thinking really means going beyond what is. The politician without anxiety, busy with the arms buildup, does not "think." But as a Christian I am obligated to expose myself to objective uncertainty: I make myself insecure through what is possible; I present myself to anxiety.

Need for God is the greatest perfection of a human person; that is a classic theological statement. What Kierkegaard has brought out is the anxiety that is concealed in the word *need.* To have no experience of anxiety, no acceptance of anxiety, means not to become human.

In a certain sense one can say that God baits us with anxiety; those who have let themselves be caught, those who have tried it, those who cannot get free of it even with the finest cleansing agents—they are hanging on God's hook.

Notes

1. Søren Kierkegaard, *The Concept of Anxiety.* Edited and translated by Reidar Thomte in collaboration with Albert B. Anderson. (Princeton, N.J.: Princeton University Press, 1980), 95.

2. Ibid., 115.

3. Ibid., 109.

4. Ibid., 155.

Rudolf Bultmann and Political Theology

Whenever I sent Rudolf Bultmann an essay, I received a postcard in reply. One of those I have kept closes: "With cordial, so to speak grandfatherly greetings." It made me quite happy at the time, because it very precisely expresses my relationship to this great theologian. I remember him with unfailing gratitude. I did not experience Rudolf Bultmann directly as a teacher, so I regard myself as his grand-daughter-student. But without him I would at that time have found no access to theology and, what says infinitely more, probably no access to faith.

Here I want to discuss the meaning of demythologizing and liberation theology's criticism of Western philosophy. It is a kind of continuation of what Bultmann did, in light of the newer discussion of myth.

I would like to present the first part, which deals with the meaning of demythologizing, in the form of biography. I come from the liberal Protestant middle class in which Kant and Goethe played a much greater role than the Bible or Luther. Intellectual doubt concerning the content of the church's teaching was, in the "enlightened" climate in which we grew up, simply a matter of course. Virgin birth, empty tomb, miracle stories, and dogmas—who could be interested in such things? There was, of course, something in this tradition that held me: Jesus Christ, this man tortured to death yet neither nihilistic nor cynical like so many people of my acquaintance after the German catastrophe. But this man from Nazareth was disguised by the church's tradition; the platitudes in Confirmation instruction, the boredom of worship services and their authoritarian claims, and finally the neo-orthodoxy encountered in religion class, which insisted that God had to be "totally other" than all our ideas. Even if there were a Christian substance, I could not recognize it in its ecclesial packaging.

In this connection—I am referring to the end of my school years, the last two years in the preparatory school I attended up to 1949—Rudolf Bultmann, whose ideas were introduced to me by his student, Professor Marie Veit, was a help to me. He was, as I learned from her, both enlightened and Christian. I did not have to surrender my intellect at the church door. He was a teacher, and I came to know him better and better through his writings as a man of impeccable honesty, a thinker in the tradition of Lessing, who would not permit himself to be cowed either by institutions like the church or by traditions like those of the Bible, and who at the same time, as I heard, was quite devout, a world-famous professor who took up the collection every Sunday for many years in the parish church in Marburg. How could the two things go together: thinking and believing, criticism and piety, reason and Christianity?

Bultmann responded to these questions with his program of demythologizing. That meant recognizing clearly that the Bible and the Christian message that followed it stem from a world marked by mythical thinking. This world view is gone, and the role that myth formerly played in explaining the world has today been taken over by science. One of Bultmann's famous statements was to the effect that: "No one can use electric light and the radio, take advantage of modern medical techniques in sickness, and at the same time believe in the world of spirits and miracles of the New Testament." Bultmann was not concerned to eliminate or dissolve the myth, but to interpret it so that the message of the Bible would also touch the children of the age of science. We cannot live partly in a scientific age and partly in a mythical one. This contradiction makes reason irresponsible and turns faith into a flight from reality. Therefore the Bible has to be "demythologized," which means to free it from the spell of mythical thinking.

In fact, I did experience Bultmann's ideas as liberating, and so did many others. Dietrich Bonhoeffer wrote in July 1942: "Bultmann has let the cat out of the bag, not only for himself, but for very many people, and I am delighted. He has dared to say what many people (I include myself) have repressed inside themselves without being able to overcome it."[1] The cat has gotten out of the mythological bag; the stories of Jesus' empty tomb and his resurrection, the idea that his resurrected form was visible and tangible, are legends, forms in which the first disciples expressed their faith in terms compatible with their worldview. If we take seriously what they wanted to say, we cannot simply parrot it; the mystery of faith and its power would then perish in the repetition, which contains within itself the repression of our doubts. And Bultmann's concern is for this mystery of faith, in which people are liberated from their past, where they tried to make themselves secure, so as to be made free for the future of love. As a teacher he continually encouraged people to devotion; as a thinker he encouraged them no less to an existence free from mythology.

Bultmann's thought was the focus of discussion up to the middle of the 1960s. He did not complete the process that began about that time, which I would call the politicization of Christian conscience. But the theology that today is as controversial as was that of Bultmann in his own time is the theology of liberation—not liberation from myth, but from material suffering, which, in a Christian view of things, not only robs the starving of hope and destroys them, but does the same to those who starve them for the sake of their own security.

Under the concept of liberation theology—to come to my second point—I include not only the Latin American theology called by this name, but a worldwide movement, carried on by many different groups, of Christians who are no longer prepared to make use of theology to justify existing injustice. It is, to take an image from its most important symbol, an exodus theology that makes the departure from each and every Egypt of oppression its own theological theme. Redemption is understood as liberation; Christ is the liberator.

To build a world in which justice will be possible, and therefore peace as well, means working toward the reign of God—a work that can never be completed but that is nonetheless indispensable. I cannot go into all the branches of this genuine theology, but I want to try to trace the lines leading from Bultmann to liberation theology, in order to arrive at some theological statements for the liberation of the rich, white middle classes of the First World as well.

The existential interpretation, with its criticism of the objectification imposed by the myth on life's fulfillment, was supported, for Bultmann and Heidegger as well, by a far-reaching critique of that Western philosophy, Greek in origin, that understood Being as being-in-itself prior to all relationship to another. The basis of Bultmann's criticism of Western philosophy was the counterposition of Hebrew and Greek thought, and in this conflict he located himself, despite all his great inner devotion to the Greeks, on the side of biblical, Hebraic thought.

We must finally learn how to think like Hebrews and stop thinking metaphysically like Greeks. Precisely this driving force plays a major role in Latin American liberation theology, based on the fact that Greek philosophy—especially, of course, Aristotelianism, which has been so influential in the West—proceeds from the idea of a Being as being-in-itself, independent of relationship to others. Western thought perceived objects as subordinated to a dominant subject, instead of developing, as did the Hebrews, an ontology of being-in-relationship.

One can understand Bultmann's unfortunate reverence for Heidegger as an attempt to find a different ontology. He did this with the aid of the philosophy that was then at his disposal, existential philosophy. This is shown by the fact that he turned for assistance, so to speak, to the one who at least had seen the problem of Western philosophy, namely this subject-object dichotomy and the domination that it conceals. If I regard Bultmann's affection for Heidigger's thinking as unfortunate, it nevertheless indicates a problem that we should take into account: It has since become evident, within liberation theology, that the consequence of this abstractive ontology of being-in-itself is that one not only regards the objects as objects, but treats them as objects. Domination and subordination are the specific Western forms in which relationships are conceived: *divide et impera*—divide and conquer.

The spirit of this philosophy of subjugation of the object by a relationless subject leads to what the Mexican liberation theologian José Miranda has analyzed, in his important book *Marx and the Bible*,[2] as a culture of injustice. I will try to recapitulate his description. The positivist idea of science, which Bultmann opposed with the tools of existential philosophy, is unmasked by Miranda as the fundamental modern principle, developed out of this relationless ontology according to which injustice, the domination of people over others, the subjugation of the object by a subject, appears as the "harmless universal principle," as Miranda says, a kind of nature, "a characteristic inherent in human existence." We are, Miranda writes, so accustomed to the injustice that consists in evaluating the work that constitutes a human life in terms of salable goods, that we consider the oppression of part of humanity to be perfectly natural and think of justice only in terms of the model established in Roman law, a model of commerce, contract, and exchange, that is, as commutative justice.

Our false ontology, in which relationship is nothing but domination, also leads us to disguise and tame the contradictoriness of the reality. Our positivist notion of science makes us blind to the deepest dimension of reality—namely, human consciousness that demands liberation. Many liberation theologians regard this as the deepest dimension of the human, which, however, is simply denied by the dominant ontology. In classical logic we learn that reality cannot be contradictory. This postulate is fulfilled by the philosophy that is born to neutralize reality, "so that it no longer approaches me, so that it no longer touches me."

This is one point at which I want to say something as a woman. It is one of the basic experiences of women who immigrate to the foreign land of the men, the universities governed and dominated by men, that they are there offered an interpretation of reality in which everything depends on neutralizing reality so that it "does not approach me, does not touch me." This philosophy with which we continually live and work is there in order to "objectify" reality. This is the source of the false scientific ideals of neutrality and objectivity that deny precisely the depth of reality and the longing of human beings for freedom and justice, as not being "objective," not worthy of scientific regard. From here come the false ideals that deny the epistemological distinction that exists between one who is sated and another who is hungry, between one who thirsts for justice and one who has an understandable interest in maintaining the present system.

Thus far José Miranda, whom I interpret in continuity and contrast to Rudolf Bultmann. Like Bultmann, he criticizes the Greek conception of history, in which there is no final goal, where contradictions are eliminated and hope is realized—which thus recognizes no eschatology—in which justice is also realized; and he criticizes this idea of history, just as Bultmann did, if perhaps not radically enough in his case. This concept of history—namely, that there is no final goal; that history goes in circles; that sometimes one group is on top, sometimes another; that a revolution consists in putting a few different people on top, who, after a short time, will do exactly the same things that were done before—this notion of reality totally rules our Western, bourgeois world. It is the absolutely controlling idea of history.

This concept of history is expressed most trivially and terribly in the common, atheistic statement: "There's nothing you can do." That sums up the impotence of the people in our country, as we saw most clearly in the peace movement. Although 78 percent of the population were against the stationing of mid-range missiles, these same people were not prepared to change their political affiliation or their thinking in accordance with their opinion on this question, which therefore remained just an opinion. They say simultaneously, "We are against them," and "There's nothing you can do." The hopelessness, the powerlessness, the submission to a fate determined from outside struck me most forcefully in these years. That is the most atheistic thing that people in our country say: "There's nothing you can do." That is believing in fate, which is the Greek idea of history. No light from the Bible whatsoever has ever penetrated this idea of history. Things just go their round, they go up and down, and the only salvation that is still offered is private and individualistic. Look out for yourself and have a few nice days—that is the solution that follows from this idea of history and this concept of reality.

Our epistemology in this connection is one of observation and distance from action. That, too, is one of the idols of science. It has nothing to do with human activity. It must be irrelevant to action and simply observe. Miranda describes it as "that quiet knowledge that characterizes a self-confident amorality." That is exactly what one finds in the German university. Truth, as Bultmann had critically remarked, is understood in Greek fashion as something observed, and not in practical Hebrew fashion as what one does with one's life. Therefore we need a more profound critique of Greek and Western philosophy, which theology has always resisted but whose domination it could not break for socioeconomic reasons. This critique will unmask the philosophy of oppression, not only the practice that regrettably does not attain to its high ideals. That is another one of those bourgeois models that we have imagined: Yes indeed, we recognize the truth and we also have high ideals, but unfortunately we cannot yet quite realize them in practice.

That is not the question! The fact is that our thinking is wrong from top to bottom, because it recognizes and cooperates with the conditions of the subject-object relationship of domination and the subjection of the majority of humanity. We live, breathe, are born and socialized into a culture of injustice, in which injustice is the highest value, to which we offer up everything we do, including the massing of armaments, in order to preserve injustice. The rape of other nations, the plundering of nature, the oppression of slaves, day laborers, workers, and the unemployed—an American expression for it is "rapism," the rape-mentality of the ruling culture—this matter-of-fact violence reflects and reproduces itself in that philosophy that has infected all of us, even if, in our conscious moral decisions, we do not join ourselves with the rapists.

The First World, whose citizens we are, is characterized by and owes its successes to: (1) an objectivizing theory of knowledge that ignores contradictions and the needs of humanity; (2) an idea of history without hope, in which hope has only a private meaning; and (3) that ontology of the subject without needs, which chooses, uses, and abandons its objects because it knows itself independent of them. Liberation theologians today are working to overcome this ontology and this theology, as Rudolf Bultmann did before them.

The term *political theology* is already almost a part of church history. My book, *Politische Theologie—Auseinandersetzung mit Rudolf Bult-mann*,[3] appeared in 1971. It grew out of the experiences of our group for "political night prayer" in Cologne starting in 1968, out of experiences in connection with the Vietnam war and the effects it had on us, and out of the student movement. It reflected the theoretical background of our praxis at the end of the sixties. Bultmann wrote me a four-page critical letter in response to that book. I would like to quote part of it:

> I agree with you that, through certain changes in social structures, the number of the forces that compel us to sin today, could be reduced. But what does it mean to sin? According to my "individualistic" understanding, one cannot speak of a sin that is brought about by the forces of the society's structures. I understand sin to be an action from person to person, for example, a lie, a breach of trust, seduction, and such things, but not a collective offense against what is commanded. In your intention, however, you are correct. But what you describe as sin, I call guilt. You do not distinguish between sin and guilt. To take your banana example: it really does make a difference whether I kill and rob a banana grower or whether I obtain the bananas through the mediation of United Fruit Company. If the latter does not pay the banana grower enough, he could always take them to court or go on strike.

I had to laugh at that, but also weep. The greatness of liberal thought is its hope, and it is a part of that heritage that we need to hold on to. This hope is absolutely naive and does not have the least contact with reality, because this banana grower, this campesino, this exploited slave, can certainly neither go on strike nor go to court. Liberal thought appears here as totally unrealistic, but at the same time it contains a demand that we cannot do without under any circumstances. Of course I take a critical and skeptical stance toward Bultmann's observations. The difference between guilt and sin cannot be so defined, in my opinion, that guilt is collective and sin is only individual. I regard that as a completely false division, and I say this precisely from my own experience and my reflection on the fate of our nation, the German question and all that it means to be a German after Auschwitz. One of the consequences I have drawn from it is just this: that it is a question of sin and that we cannot absolve ourselves of personal sin in the face of six million murdered Jews. My whole consciousness of sin, if I may so speak, rests on the collective events that are happening in my country, in my city, in my group. I want to say frankly that the individual sins of which I accuse myself and which of course I recognize in my life occupy, nevertheless, a much smaller space. That is simply my experience. The things I suffer over, for which I beg forgiveness, for which I need forgiving, are the terrible, catastrophic deeds that we as a society are doing today.

What separates me at this point from Bultmann can be summed up in one word: Auschwitz. My attempt to do theology is shaped by the knowledge that I live after Auschwitz. Bultmann, on the other hand, thinks within the context of a bourgeois understanding of science as timeless and objectivizing. Perhaps his existential interpretation was not existential enough really to deliver him from the ontology of oppression.

The expression *political theology*, as a description of what we—I am thinking of Jürgen Moltmann, Johannes Baptist Metz, and myself—were then trying to do, was too cautious, too formal, and too ambiguous a concept, even though it did represent a beginning for us in the First World. In the meantime a better term has been given us by Latin America. Today I understand my theology as an attempt to do liberation theology in the First World.

But in the process, my understanding of myth has also changed. Within the theology of liberation, myth looks different, depending on whether it is being used by the rich as a distraction or by the poor as the bread of hope. For about two years now, the question of the meaning of myth has reappeared in our culture, inspired by film, fantasy literature, and the plastic arts. And this discussion is new in relation to the one Bultmann was dealing with, because science, which was supposed to take the place of myth, is no longer able to bear the burden of explaining and shaping the world, at least not for those of us who are most sensitive.

I need a different language from that of explanation, definition, and criticism in order to express with any clarity at all what is at stake. And that is the point at which I believe I aspire to go a little beyond Bultmann—not backward into biblicist naiveté, into a pre-Enlightenment world, but passing through the Enlightenment into a new language, which we are working on today in liberation theology, a language we are searching for and one we really need. Great theology, certainly, has always practiced narration and prayer. And I remember a lecture by Bultmann that drew rapt attention from all of us. He insisted, and always made clear, that speech from the lectern in the university is not the same as preaching in church—that they are two very different things. Someone said to him in the discussion: "But what you just did was exactly like prayer for me." And it really was. He did not want to accept it, but his theology was better than his own opinion of it, and it had the quality of great theology: it spoke the different languages of religion with the passion of the absolute. The languages of religion are narrative, prayer, and argument.

We need mythical stories, we need a confession of sin, an understanding of ourselves, an examination of conscience, and we need the reflective argument for these three levels of religious language, of which theology is only one, while the other two have not yet found their place. What we are working on today, especially in feminist theology, is an attempt to reconcile these three levels of language again with one another, in order to liberate theology from its isolated situation in which it is headless, understanding itself as mere argument and no longer having a share in the language of prayer and story. A liberated theology will take part in the three various theological media, the three forms of religious language.

I think that even though Bultmann practiced this restriction of theology, the nature of the subject often pushed him beyond the restriction of decapitated argument so that he prayed in his theology. Kierkegaard is for me one of the greatest theologians, because he speaks these three languages in his own way: he narrates, he prays, and he argues. He does not let himself be forced onto a single level of language. In this sense I think that theology must have a share in all these levels.

Meaningful theology, on the contrary, invites the return of myth. Narrative or story is sought out and not banished as impure. That is also one of the criteria of liberation theology: that it tries to think from the point of view of the poor, the blacks, or women, and tries to bring in the reality of their lives by means of story. Witnesses appear in the major ecumenical conferences. The model of German scholarship that dominated the world churches for so long is by this time totally finished. It is thoroughly clear that genuine recognition of truth happens in ways different from those by which it has been customary to organize a scholarly conference. That is evident in the ecumenical movement, when Domitila, a woman from the mining district of Bolivia, gets up and tells how she lives and what she has experienced, and when these participants, living witnesses to the life people are leading today, make up the strongest part of such a conference—as was the case, for example, in Vancouver. What she said cannot be summarized in a communiqué; prayer and story refuse to be captured in this form of communication—they would freeze to death.

I think we are presently ill at ease within this new discussion of myth, and we are working on that in liberation theology. When I ask myself what Rudolf Bultmann would have said about this new discussion, I think it would probably have been both yes and no. No to the myth, if it represents merely a return to the irrational: learned, artistically important, and at the same time a complete denial of whatever we may have thought of as enlightenment. No to a myth whose power we experience with a shudder, but whose content we are no longer able to distinguish in a critical manner. Demythologization is and remains a means for obtaining a clear view of the lords of this world.

Yes to the myth if it represents a post-naive turning toward something, a third step that leads from naive faith through liberating, demythologizing critique to a reappropriation of the hope promised through the myth for all people. Yes, if in the myth the action of God for the world, which otherwise remains invisible and, in my experience, is more and more difficult to express, shines forth: that the child in the manger is really stronger than the wielders of power and their child-murdering soldiers, and that the Jesus who is tortured to death is living among us today. No to a myth of power that demands subjugation and adoration of the strongest. Yes to a myth of love, which declares that the world is apt for reconciliation and that we all can be healed.

Notes

1. Quoted in Eberhard Bethge, *Dietrich Bonhoeffer: Eine Biographie* (München: Kaiser, 1967), 800.

2. José P. Miranda, *Marx and the Bible. A Critique of the Philosophy of Oppression,* trans. by John Eagleson (Maryknoll, N.Y.: Orbis, 1974).

3. English trans.: *Political Theology,* trans. with an introduction by John Shelley (Philadelphia: Fortress, 1974).

America, as a nation and a people, has stood
in her brief history as the mightiest (and perhaps the last) great home of the FAITH. She
is known to the peoples of the world as a
"Christian nation."

It follows naturally that she and her people
are the special target of Satan as he seeks to
devour the planet and everyone on it. . . .

—*Christian Voice Newsletter*[1]

Christofascism

Christian Voice is a New Right organization in Pasadena, California,
that works much like the Moral Majority to activate fundamentalist
Christians and especially their pastors politically. What has established
itself in America since the beginning of the eighties as the New Right
is a weaving together of goals of the ultraconservative Old Right with
the pragmatic strategies of liberals, making skillful use of the media.
In letters like the one cited above, addressed to "Dear Brother in
Christ," in television programs and conventions, the faithful members
are urged again and again to "put feet to their prayers," that is, to
give money and to write to their government representatives, television stations, school principals, and officeholders.

Prayer chains are often combined with telephone trees—for example, to defeat progressive senators or block liberal laws. In this way
a law for equal rights for homosexuals was headed off in Minnesota
in 1977: "In less than twenty-four hours, 100 prayer chains were
contacted, and hundreds of phone calls were made to key legislators."[2]
Without the media and their technicians, without the electronic
church, the development of this extreme New Right would be unimaginable. I will begin by describing my own observations from
viewing religious television, then offer some interpretation in light of
the contemporary background in the United States, and finally attempt
a theological critique.

I. The Electronic Church

Europeans can scarcely imagine the size, financial power, and growth
of the religious television movement. In the United States it is no

longer a matter of old-fashioned tent meetings in the great tradition of rhetorical preaching. The new evangelists are creatures of television, cool transmitters of the message. They do not shout; they speak softly, skillfully, and movingly. They are perfect masters of the medium: "These people sell their product," said a young born-again man in an advertising agency, seated between images of cowboys and sensuous women, "and we are here for our own purpose: we are selling the gospel." Can the gospel be sold like soap, Bahama vacations, and sex?

There are a couple of simple recipes for spreading the new religion. The most important is success: show the successful that religion really helps! On almost every program there are people who give testimony—an interview with the manager who had been an alcoholic, a talk with the hit singer who was shy. Things were just terrible for me, they relate, I didn't know what to do, my marriage was going badly, my boss was giving me suspicious looks, I was in a crisis! Until I found Jesus. Accepted him as my Lord. (The organ music swells gently.) How wonderful everything is now, praise God! Success in business, in marriage. Wealth, fame, and power are the basic American values that are unconsciously addressed, simply through the aura of the persons who appear on the screen. Just as cigarette advertising speaks to our unconscious longing for green forests, rushing water, and clear air, so the well-groomed, rich, white man on the screen offers us promises: Take this cigarette, take God, and it will go as well for you as it has for me.

One agency is called Seeds of Faith. It explains the unbelievable financial success of the electronic church, far greater than that of the traditional denominations. The message here is: Give in order to receive. If you give God something today, if you really sacrifice something, he will repay you your gift tomorrow, and a "heaped-up measure" (Luke 6:38) will be yours. First give, and then you can expect miracles in your life. But what if they don't happen? You didn't receive anything from God in return? Then you must not have given enough! Give more, you'll see. . . . And the simple fact that religious programs of this kind go on and on, paid for by the donations of their viewers, is a proof that prayers are heard. The connection between money and religion, being rich and being pious, is no longer even a subject for reflection. The anwer of the religious Right to the question of what religion and faith are all about is simple and striking: "It works."

It is a well-known sales technique à la Madison Avenue: offer small gifts—pamphlets, religious books, Bibles, pins, American flags—all free just for calling in. Jerry Falwell gave away two million pins inscribed "Jesus first" in one year. Free, no cost. While the music soars and a prayer begins, the telephone number appears again and again on the screen. Anyone who calls gets plugged into the sales system. The electronic church is not only television, it is a sales technique combining television, telephone calls, letters, address lists. Once you get the free gift, you will be bombarded with letters and folders. The "great need that can only be answered by your own personal gift" is explained, and the addressed envelope for the check is enclosed. If nothing comes back after two or three letters, the computer spits your name out again. If you do give anything, more letters arrive, sorted according to the size of your gift: in cream-colored envelopes for those who have pledged ten dollars a month, rust-colored for those who give five hundred dollars or more.

Every call and every letter is answered personally. The scientifically tested method is perfect. Computers sort the mail according to marriage, alcohol, or other problems, and write long, personal letters, indistinguishable from real ones; the stamps are stuck on. Everyone who, attracted by the television program, calls the prayer number receives advice and Bible verses; name and address go into the computer. Later you receive a prayer list to check off: alcohol, anxiety, arthritis, asthma . . . for every problem from A to Z, a personal prayer from a volunteer helper.

Jerry Falwell, a fundamentalist pastor with his own Baptist congregation in Lynchburg, Virginia, got into business with his television program, "The Old Time Gospel Hour": he receives checks for $50,000 a week. Whom is he reaching? These are the people for whom the American dream has not become a reality, people who have been impoverished by inflation, isolated suburbanites, politically frustrated little people. The Moral Majority promises them that everything will be fine again . . . the way it was. America will be Number One again, sexuality under control, criminality abolished. The values of the Moral Majority are "decency, home and family, biblical morality, and free enterprise, the great ideals that are the cornerstone of this great nation." The continually repeated message is simple, and it is hammered into insecure and unsuccessful people with the confidence of the successful. Jesus loves you. The moral strength of the nation has been weakened. Give Jesus your heart, and he will give you what you want. An optimistic message: Be positive!

II. The Theologizing of Politics and the End of Secularization

After the attack on Grenada, in the fall of 1982, Robert McAfee Brown, a leading Presbyterian theologian, wrote an open letter to Christians outside America, in which he showed how much "civilian control of the military (one of our most cherished traditions) has been replaced by military control of the civilian population (one of the best tests for the beginning of a turn toward military fascism)." Brown pointed out how both of the most important instruments of American democracy, Congress and the free press, had been set aside during the occupation of Grenada "in the name of the ideology of national security." The military-political doctrine of national security has largely replaced the older political values and convictions of democracy, freedom of the press, and human rights; instead, "national security" has become the foundation of politics.

This program has an external military side, but it also has an internal religious and cultural side. The political debate in the United States is, according to my observation, being increasingly theologized. It is not mere ideological positions, but two religions that are fighting with one another. This means the end of the liberal era and especially the end of its thesis about the secularization of society. The steps taken by Harvard theologian Harvey Cox, for example, from his *The Secular City* in the sixties to *Religion in the Secular City* in the eighties, testify to the survival and the new polarizing of religion. What is new is the alliance of the theological element with the extreme political Right.

The historical perspective of neoconservatism is a comprehensive critique of those liberals who, twenty years ago, still maintained the secular and optimistic notion that capitalism would eventually free the world from want and misery. This illusion collapsed in the sixties, both in the Third World and in the ghettos of poverty in North America. The great revolutionary liberation movements in the Third World were repressed by coups, economic boycotts, CIA plots, and—when necessary—wars. But the challenges behind them and the injustice of the existing economic order were not perceived. The self-confidence of the United States was deeply wounded in the early seventies by the loss of the Vietnam war and by the oil crisis. The extreme Right has a ready answer for all that: it demands a politics of strength, not of justice. The conservatives united by blaming liberalism for all the problems it neither could solve nor wanted to solve. The welfare state had caused the collapse of the Protestant work ethic; a weak program of national defense had allowed the Soviet Union to "win" the arms race. And finally, the women's movement had "destroyed" the American family.

Ronald Reagan himself referred to pornography, drug addiction, and the collapse of the family, once "the cornerstone of our society," as the symptoms of the moral decline of the United States. According to his view of history: "All our material prosperity and all our influence are founded on our faith in God and the basic values that follow from that faith."

Americans are urged to believe in the moral superiority of the United States, a faith that stands in marked contrast to the political and cultural isolation of the United States today in almost every international forum, and to the still growing anti-Americanism resulting from the militarization of its satellite states. Reagan of course insisted that he would never cease "to pray that the leaders [of the Soviet Union], like so many of their own people, would come to know the liberating nature of faith in God." But this rhetoric does not bear the least relation to the new strategic plans for total destruction of the enemy through a lightning war, as developed in the Pentagon's document "Airland 2000." The new American chauvinism and the unchecked militarization of the earth and the heavens require inner, religious armaments; they need James Robinson's television show, "Wake Up, America!" in which Christians are instructed to articulate their faith politically. Viewers who respond to Jerry Falwell's television preaching receive letters challenging them to become Faith Partner Crusaders.

The second value in neoconservative religion is work, hard work: no sympathy is wasted on those who do not work. In the context of Reagan's economic policies, that meant no health care for the masses of elderly, sick, and so-called unemployables. The denial of reality, the refusal to acknowledge certain things that do not accord with the ideology, is in my opinion characteristic of aggressive neoconservatism. In Jerry Falwell's book, *Listen, America!* Milton Friedman, the ultraconservative economic theorist of the Chicago school, appears in the role of evangelist. Every form of welfare, aid, or solidarity with the weaker is regarded not only as counterproductive, but also as anti-biblical. This religious legitimation of capitalism in its most brutal forms has never before existed even in the United States. "The system of free enterprise is clearly prescribed in the Bible, in the Proverbs of

Solomon. Jesus Christ makes clear that the work ethic is part of his plan for mankind. Private property is biblical. Business competition is biblical. Ambitious and successful business practice is clearly prescribed as part of God's plan for his people."[3]

The third value in the new Christofascist civil religion is the family and, within it, the role of the woman. Being religious means keeping women in the place ordained for them by God. A patriarchal ideology of the family complements an attitude of extreme hostility toward labor unions and a rejection of all social measures. Reagan was a master at playing on the deep-seated anxieties of people caught up in massive technological change. He exploited their fear of inflation and of the loss of jobs and turned it toward a different point—namely, sexuality. It is not the nuclear bomb that threatens our survival; it is love between two men or two women that endangers everything we have achieved! The moral scandal of our time is not the starvation of a million children in the Third World, thanks to our masterly economic planning, but the abortion of unborn life! Unemployment is not the problem; pornography is!

III. Theological Critique

People are told repeatedly that pornography, homosexuality, and promiscuity go with secular humanism, satanism, and communism; these last three are lumped together without distinction. The primitiveness of the argumentation is scandalous. For believers who are dependent on authority and in search of something to hold on to, religion is instrumentalized in order to engender hate, to lead them into battle, into crusades. It is this instrumentalization of religion for completely different ends that inspired me to formulate a concept that needs some further clarification: Christofascism.

In our public discussion the concept of fascism has been almost completely reduced to totalitarianism, even by the moderate Right. All the other essential elements of German fascism in particular, such as its racist mania and its militarism, are dismissed as irrelevant. According to the strange logic of some of our guardians of democracy, President Reagan, because he was democratically elected—albeit by only 27 percent of the U.S. population—simply cannot have any fascist tendencies. In this debate the electoral process as such takes on a sacrosanct quality, as if no democratic country had ever stumbled into genocide (in Southeast Asia, for example). Democracy, in this way of thinking, is a purely formal structure, and its lack of political substance, so evident in its militarism, racism, sexism, and in the neo-colonial exploitation of the peoples of the Third World, is of no further interest.

But the most dangerous thing about Christofascist religion is precisely that it is not compulsory, nor is it brought about in totalitarian fashion by violence. It is a matter of what critical Americans call "soft fascism": chauvinistic nationalism, militarization of one's own land and all its dependent countries, the still-unconquered racism that expresses itself also in the reintroduction of capital punishment, the celebration of violence in films—to the extent that the victims are described as "communists"—all these fascist tendencies are not imposed by violence, but instead are freely "bought." And one of the essential differences between this and European fascism is, in my judgment, the geopolitical fact that nowadays the concentration camps are not close to Weimar or Munich, but are far away: in El Salvador, in the Philippines, in South Africa, and wherever the great world power permits or encourages torture and murder, or has done so in the past.

These connections—the internal and external brutalizations—must remain as invisible as possible, and here too the religious-ideological support system of the Western world plays a key role. It leads the population to a freely chosen acceptance of militarism. And militarism, that is, the absolute priority of military ends over all other public obligations, is in fact a substantial criterion for Hitler-style fascism. "Whoever votes for Hitler, votes for war," could be read on the walls of houses in Berlin in 1932. Anyone who questions American militarism—like the Catholic bishops or some cautious voices in the National Council of Churches—is demonized by the religious Right and called an aide to the communists.

Within the Moral Majority, excessive nationalism has increasingly taken on the features of anti-Semitism as well. Dr. Bailie Smith, president of the Southern Baptist Convention, declared at a meeting, "God Almighty does not hear the prayer of a Jew."[4] Add to that an image of the enemy that is not troubled by any kind of knowledge or experience, as clearly expressed by Ronald Reagan when he called the Soviet Union "the root of all evil." This remark recalls the Nazi slogan, "The Jews are our misfortune."

Everyday anticommunism is unimaginably blind; I myself was in a discussion in a middle-class church where, when I mentioned a friend of mine who is a pastor in East Berlin, a woman shouted at me: "That can't be so; there are no pastors in the East, they are all in concentration camps and the churches have been burned!" This ideological mixture of nationalism, militarism, family ideology, hostility to working people, and blind hatred of communism is compounded with Christianity by the religious Right; the Christian religion is made the vehicle of these ideologies, so that in many cases people who are outside the churches have no conception of Christianity except in this Christofascist form. The deepest meaning of the Christian religion is conformed and subordinated to fears and threatening lies, to hate and the will to destroy.

In a theological perspective it is evident that the content of this fascist religion contradicts the message of the Jewish-Christian tradition. The God of the prophets did not preach the nation-state, but community between strangers and natives. The apostle Paul did not base the justification of sinners on the Protestant work ethic, but on grace, which appears for young and old, for diligent and for lazy people! And Jesus did not make the family the central value of human life, but the solidarity of those deprived of their rights. The most important norms of the Moral Majority are not contained in Christian faith, as we can see from the many critical remarks against the family that appear in the gospels. It is characteristic of Christofascism that it cuts off all the roots that Christianity has in the Old Testament, in the Jewish Bible. No word about justice, no mention of the poor, whom God comes to aid, very little about guilt and suffering. No hope for the messianic reign. Hope is completely individualized and reduced to personal success. Jesus, cut loose from the Old Testament, becomes a sentimental figure. The empty repetition of his name works like a drug: it changes nothing and nobody. Therefore, since not everybody can be successful, beautiful, male, and rich, there have to be hate objects who can take the disappointment on themselves. Jesus, who suffered hunger and poverty, who practiced solidarity with the oppressed, has nothing to do with this religion.

At a mass meeting a thousand voices shouted: "I love Jesus" and "I love America"—it was impossible to distinguish the two. This kind of religion knows the cross only as a magical symbol of what he has done for us, not as the sign of the poor man who was tortured to death as a political criminal, like thousands today who stand up for his truth in El Salvador. This is a God without justice, a Jesus without a cross, an Easter without a cross—what remains is a metaphysical Easter Bunny in front of the beautiful blue light of the television screen, a betrayal of the disappointed, a miracle weapon in service of the mighty.

Notes

1. Quotations are from Peggy L. Shriver, *The Bible Vote: Religion and the New Right* (New York: Pilgrim Press, 1981), and from Flo Conway and Jim Siegelmann, *Holy Terror: The Fundamentalist War on America's Freedoms in Religion, Politics and Our Private Lives* (New York: Dell, 1984).

2. Intercessors for America newsletter, quoted in Shriver, *Bible Vote,* 28.

3. Jerry Falwell, *Listen, America!* (Garden City, N.Y.: Doubleday, 1980).

4. Quoted in Shriver, *Bible Vote,* 29.

For Walter Jens

Civil
Disobedience

VARIATIONS ON A THEME FROM
HENRY DAVID THOREAU

In this essay I want to honor a democratic German writer and to take possession, for him, for myself, and for my readers, of a tradition that we will need most urgently in the coming struggles for peace. I will try to let one of the fathers of the "other America" speak, to improve Germans' very narrow idea of democracy, and to understand *civil disobedience* as an obligation.

The first difficulty I encountered in this was translating the idea into German. It is not only a linguistic problem but a question of lack of tradition, a shortage of experience and democratic under-development. What is civil disobedience? Is it "civilian" resistance, that is, resistance that is carried out by normal citizens in contrast to military resistance with weapons? Is "disobedience to the state" the proper translation? In the dictionary I find under *civil disobedience:* The refusal to obey certain laws or governmental demands for the purpose of influencing legislation or government policy, characterized by the employment of such nonviolent techniques as boycotting, pick-eting, and nonpayment of taxes."[1] I can best express the thesis of this essay in Thoreau's and Gandhi's language: Civil disobedience is a necessary form of *ahimsa*, the love of all living things. But how can

I say that in German in such a way that it will motivate our political actions?

Henry David Thoreau (1817–1862) lived for two years beside Walden Pond in a wooden hut he built with his own hands, a freely chosen withdrawal from the world of work and civilization, an experiment with himself, a protest against the "restless, nervous, bustling, trivial Nineteenth Century." "I went to the woods because I wished to live deliberately, to front only the essential facts of life, and see if I could not learn what it had to teach, and not, when I came to die, discover that I had not lived."[2] Thoreau's masterpiece, *Walden, or Life in the Woods,* grew out of his journals from this period; from this time also stems the essay on disobedience, whose original title was "Resistance to Civil Government."

I want to recount three stories from Thoreau's life that moved me to take this crazy guy from Massachusetts into my heart. The first is from the time when he was a teacher in the Academy of his hometown of Concord, after his studies at Harvard College. "The directors were upset that Thoreau made no use of corporal punishment, which was regarded as indispensable for discipline. He was reprimanded for this. His reaction was characteristic: he called a half dozen students forward, gave each of them a swat with the ruler and quit his job."[3]

The second notable story concerns Thoreau's reaction to the death of Captain John Brown, an active resistance fighter against slavery. Brown, who had led a group helping slaves to escape via the "Underground Railroad" and had assembled weapons for his guerrilla action at Harper's Ferry, Virginia, was captured, tried, and subsequently hanged on December 2, 1859. His execution touched Thoreau, who had taken a clear position in favor of Brown and called on others to do likewise (in his address, "A Plea for Captain John Brown"), as did scarcely any other event in his life. Whenever Brown's name was mentioned, Thoreau's hands clenched. After this shock he became bedridden, succumbing to the tuberculosis of which he died on May 2, 1862. He wrote of Brown's death: ". . . not for a day or two did I even *hear* that he was *dead,* and not after any number of days shall I believe it. Of all the men who were said to be my contemporaries, it seemed to me that John Brown was the only one who *had not died. . . .* I meet him at every turn. He is more alive than ever he was. . . . He is no longer working in secret. He works in public and in the clearest light that shines on this land."[4]

The third episode is Thoreau's experience in jail, the occasion for his essay on resistance. During his stay at Walden Pond, Thoreau occasionally went to Concord. One day, as he was on his way to the shoemaker, he was arrested, because for four years past he had not paid his poll tax, as a protest against the war with Mexico and the toleration of slavery, especially the latter after the fugitive slave law went into effect. Thoreau was in jail only one night because—to his regret—a concerned aunt paid the tax for him, but this experience clarified his thinking and inspired him to write the essay on resistance that later was distributed like a textbook by Gandhi and was discussed by French resistance fighters and English labor theorists. "Under a government which imprisons any unjustly, the true place for a just man is also a prison. . . . It is there that the fugitive slave, and the Mexican prisoner on parole, and the Indian come to plead the wrongs of his race, should find them; on that separate, but more free and honorable ground, where the State places those who are not *with* her but *against* her,—the only house in a slave-state in which a free man can abide with honor."[5]

This idea, that prison is the home of freedom in a system of oppression, runs through the whole movement of the "other America" even to the present day.

In 1976 I participated in an action with the Berrigan brothers, in which we went to the Pentagon to protest the arms race through symbolic acts and the breaking of rules. In a meeting before the action the question arose: Who at that time planned or wanted to be arrested? A friend of mine, who had just accepted a college teaching position, said that his students would not learn anything from his being arrested, because they didn't know him well enough yet. Daniel Berrigan contradicted him sharply: When would they ever learn anything, then? Wouldn't his absence, his being in jail, make clearer to them than anything else ever could what was really at stake? Wasn't not-teaching really the strongest method of teaching? Could his students ever really understand anything as long as he was free?

At that time I did not yet know of Thoreau and my knowledge of Gandhi was still quite superficial. I did not understand the mystique of prison, that it can be the place for a human being in an inhuman world. I had not yet comprehended the strategy that consists of using disobedience, breaking of rules, and other forms of resistance to cause the state to throw more and more citizens into jail. I had not asked the question clearly enough: In a violent, militaristic state, how can we get beyond protest and exercise resistance? I use the word *militarism* here in the usual dictionary sense. It is defined as "1. a strong military spirit or policy. 2. the principle or policy of maintaining a large military establishment."[6] Both definitions apply to the present superpowers and their satellites.

"How," Thoreau asked in 1848, "does it become a man to behave toward this American government to-day? I answer that he cannot without disgrace be associated with it. I cannot for an instant recognize that political organization as *my* government which is the *slave's* government also."[7] Thoreau's political themes were the war that the United States conducted against Mexico from 1846 to 1848, and slavery, the eradication of which was the goal of the abolitionists. The provocation in Thoreau's thought, his "anti-Americanism," to use a slogan of the current West German government, has not become less through historical distance. With the increased demand of the state, in the wake of the Second Industrial Revolution, for obedience, subjection, and regimentation of all areas of life, Thoreau's provocation has rather increased: present decisions by the power elites intrude even more catastrophically into the lives of individuals. The power elite that assembles in Brussels under the name NATO has more to say about the lives of my children than anyone I could elect. My variation on Thoreau's statement quoted above would be: "I cannot for an instant recognize that political organization as my government which is a government of nuclear slavery also."

This is no artificial parallel of my own invention between the old slavery based on race and the new one based on military technology. It is the tradition of that "other America," so reluctantly recognized by our media, the America that stretches from Thoreau to Martin Luther King, César Chavez, Dorothy Day, and Daniel Berrigan. Such people make up the new abolitionists around the Sojourners circle in Washington who recognize the arms buildup as the crime corresponding to slavery. They understand the escalation of terror, the preparation for the nuclear holocaust, the replacement of politics by militarism, and the crime against the poor in their own country and in the Third World as the new form of slavery under which we are living. Enslaved, because in the meantime more than half of our financial resources and raw materials have been brought as sacrifices to the Moloch; enslaving, because it is the intention of our present militarism to let the poor starve so that the rich can continue to amass more riches undisturbed.

Henry Thoreau was a crazy man who would not beat children. In our schools, children are no longer beaten with sticks, only with grades. He was not prepared to pay taxes for a war of conquest; we pay for something we call "defense." He envisioned a different kind of life. This desire to be independent of all possessions he called *simplicity.* "The opportunities of living are diminished in proportion as what are called the 'means' are increased. The best thing a man can do for his culture when he is rich is to endeavour to carry out those schemes which he entertained when he was poor."[8]

Discovering Thoreau means getting involved in a discussion about real and false needs. That is just what is necessary for a culture of peace that is not built on the exploitation of others and the plundering of the earth. What at first only sounds individualistic and harmless, namely, reducing one's own needs, has something to do with the peace that is not built on militarism. Thoreau's influence does not rest on his writing; he is not one of the great ones as far as finished works are concerned, nor as regards style and expression. His strength is in his existential experiment: finding out for himself what we really need in order to live, what is superfluous, what is morally unacceptable, namely, war and slavery. It is the same love of life that Gandhi later called *ahimsa* that made Thoreau's "life in the woods" possible, as well as his political resistance to slavery.

How can this all-embracing love of life express itself in a democracy that is erected on a kind of moral reductionism, on a mediocrity that does not wish to do wrong but permits it to be done? How can love of justice be combined with the idea of majoritarian democracy? "There are thousands who are *in opinion* opposed to slavery and to the war, who yet in effect do nothing to put an end to them."[9] Thoreau criticizes those who are satisfied to have an "opinion." He calls for a "deliberate and practical denial of [government] authority."[10] He counts on alert and active minorities that the government will have to take into account. His political hope is founded on this conscious and active "wise" minority.

The difficulty for him—and certainly for us—is that the minority itself is crippled by a quantitative notion of democracy. "Men generally, under such a government as this, think that they ought to wait until they have persuaded the majority to alter [the laws]."[11] But this waiting, this mere having-a-different-opinion, this lovely democratic faith in the strength of arguments, in the power of *persuasion,* is not enough. In a democratically legitimated system of injustice that justifies war and slavery, Thoreau attempts to redefine the minority: it is not sufficient to wait and to persuade. "A minority is powerless while it conforms to the majority; it is not even a minority then; but it is irresistible when it clogs by its whole weight. If the alternative is to keep all just men in prison, or give up war and slavery, the State will not hesitate which to choose." [12] Was Thoreau overoptimistic? He believed that the state would free itself from the system of injustice and declare it "politically impossible" because every community depends on the cooperation of the conscious and active minority.

The decisive step is only taken when the minority does not wait for the next election, but immediately renounces its obedience in face of democratically legitimated injustice. Conscience cannot be delayed. "It is not desirable to cultivate a respect for the law, so much as for the right." [13] Therefore Thoreau called on those "who call themselves abolitionists . . . effectually [to] withdraw their support, both in person and property, from the government of Massachusetts. . . ." [14]

Early in 1982 the archbishop of Seattle, Raymond Hunthausen, declared that he would withhold half of his income tax because he did not want to participate in preparation for a nuclear war, "the global crucifixion of Jesus." That is an encouraging sign of resistance, of civil disobedience, and more will follow. We misunderstand such signs and the tradition they address when we say they are "only moral gestures." Whatever can seriously be called "moral" always has political character and is relevant to real power struggles. Marxist critics of nonviolent resistance were often blind to the morality that was their own guide, as if political change could consist in the mere transfer of power from one ruling elite to another, as if the question of values, such as justice, were simply left to one side.

Thoreau is a moralist; for him, compromise with a formally democratic justification of war and slavery is impossible. Instead, he draws the anarchistic conclusion: in refusal of every kind of cooperation with government power, even when it is democratically legitimated; in action now, without delay; in a minority consciousness that does not consist merely in thinking differently, but in acting and living differently. What can the resistance and peace movements of today learn from him? I would like at this point simply to pose an unavoidable question or two.

What if the majority in the Western nations, incited to anticommunist attitudes and blinded by consumerism, still wants guns *and* butter? Will words, written material, demonstrations, education for peace, and protests be enough? Don't we need a more pointed language: action and the willingness to suffer? What have we learned from the civil disobedience in Wyhl, Brokdorf, and at the western runway at Frankfurt airport[15]—how much resistance has been made possible by those actions, and how much was destroyed? And finally: What does it mean to have "more" democracy, as we are happy to say we have in contrast to our Eastern neighbors, if it does not bring us more peace? If nuclear pacifism is the moral minimum today, the consequence is an "obligation to civil disobedience" to the state that continues to offer us war and nuclear slavery as thinkable realities.

Notes

1. *The Random House Dictionary of the English Language,* 2d ed. (New York: Random House, 1987).

2. Henry David Thoreau, *Walden, or Life in the Woods, and On the Duty of Civil Disobedience,* with an afterword by Perry Miller (New York: New American Library, 1960, rev. ed. 1980); from *Walden,* 66.

3. Ibid., Afterword, 74.

4. H. D. Thoreau, "The Last Days of John Brown," *Reform Papers,* ed. Wendell Glick (Princeton, N.J.: Princeton University Press, 1973), 152–53.

5. H. D. Thoreau, "Civil Disobedience," in *Great Short Works of Henry David Thoreau,* ed. with an introduction by Wendell Glick (New York, San Francisco, and London: Harper & Row, 1982), 144–45.

6. *Random House Dictionary.*

7. "Civil Disobedience," *Great Short Works,* 137.

8. Ibid., 146.

9. Ibid., 139.

10. Ibid., 142.

11. Ibid.

12. Ibid., 145.

13. Ibid., 135.

14. Ibid., 143.

15. Wyhl and Brockdorf are sites of nuclear power plants where strong resistance arose. The extension of the Frankfurt airport destroyed a recreation area in favor of a military and business need; ten thousand ecopacifists tried in vain to stop it.

God Is
All-Sharing

Can an enlightened person still believe? Why do we need mythical stories and symbols if their contents could today be unlocked and adapted in different ways? What does faith mean, if its essential experiences, such as that of knowing oneself to be sheltered in fundamental trust and of living in an unshakable love toward all creatures, need no religious and mythical language? Is enlightened and commonsense language not sufficient for an enlightened consciousness?

No, a merely rational language is not enough. It is too small for our needs. It explains, but it does not satisfy. It illuminates—although seldom—but it does not warm. It defines, sets limits, criticizes, makes distinctions possible, but the most important thing that we as human beings can do, even and especially with our language, namely communicate, is not the special purpose of this language. At best, enlightenment leaves us room in which to share life with one another. At best, the language of enlightenment protects the time and place where we touch the holiness of life and impart it to one another. It is a defense against the destruction of that life. It forbids us to make an image or a likeness or an ideology of God—and that is absolutely necessary. It helps us to see that neither the "pressure of circumstances" nor the "total market" nor "security" is the unquestionable final reality to which we may subordinate everything else. But the language of enlightenment does not tell us what it means to love God above all things.

I have to express myself in an immediately religious manner at this point, because we need images and myths in order to name our most important experiences, our fears and desires. This is a risky business, because there is such a crowd of false myths and false religions around us. There is a discussion going on nowadays on the subject of myth, inspired by films, fantasy literature, and the arts, that may well indicate that the end of the European Enlightenment is in sight. Francis Ford Coppola's film *Apocalypse Now* (1979) may serve as a negative example. The historical reality of the Vietnam war was made the basis of an aesthetic re-mythologizing in this film. The historical reality is that a major power attacked a nation of rice farmers that was trying to free itself from its colonial masters. The mythicizing film shows how some obsessed men—lonely, misunderstood techno-heroes—rush toward a tragic fate in the jungle, to the strains of Wagnerian music! It seems as if the question of truth can no longer be asked within the historical world, and as if it were completely impossible to answer it with the aid of science or scholarship; a new search for myth and (in the broadest sense of the word) religious assurance is beginning.

This discussion is new in the sense that science, which was supposed to replace myth, is no longer able to bear the burden of explaining and shaping the world. Together with the limits of growth, the limits of science and its social responsibility have become visible. In this crisis of science, which neither the theologian Rudolf Bultmann nor his contemporary Bertolt Brecht had anticipated, the question of myth is being posed anew. Is myth, the story of the penetration of divine forces into human reality, necessary to describe the future or even any kind of hope for the world?

In what follows I will not distinguish between myth, religion, and poetry, although this distinction is historically justified. In the present situation, however, it is of no use to us. As a writer I work with theological material as artists work with stone, wire, wood, or other materials. The Bible, the lives of the saints, the history of the church—which essentially means systematic theological reflection, since the institution has not succeeded, in spite of intense effort, in destroying the gospel—these are the materials I need in order to shed some light on a dark and confused context. I will give an example to show clearly how I work.

In Mutlangen, in September 1983, there was a blockade of the installation for mass conflagration that was then being planned and has since been built. It poured rain during the night, and my group crouched, shivering, under a tent cloth. A middle-aged woman rode up on a bicycle and brought us hot tea. She said she was a substitute teacher in a nearby town. She could not make an open commitment to the peace movement, as her sister had done, because she would lose her job. "But since I favor more practical measures anyway, I brought you tea."

I was very happy about this incident. Later on, I tried to express my pleasure to some other people. They listened and found it "very nice." But that was not what I had experienced. I had not been able to explain myself clearly in the language of facts. This woman was one of the "little people": humble in appearance, timid in her movements, disadvantaged in comparison to her sister, constantly in danger of doing something wrong in her job—a damaged person. And yet she rode her bicycle through the night, in the rain, to bring us tea. Finally a story from the New Testament occurred to me: about the widow whom Jesus watched as she dropped "two copper coins" into the treasury (Mark 12:41-44). "This poor widow has put in more than all those who are contributing to the treasury. For they all contributed out of their abundance; but she out of her poverty has put in everything she had, her whole food for today" (12:44).

When I thought of the poor widow in the gospel, I understood the woman in Mutlangen better. I was better able to describe the joy she represented for us. Why should an old story from the Jesus tradition help me to write today? What does mythical-narrative language contribute? Something that, although it is contained in my empirical reality, is usually not visible. I use the gospel, or other religious traditions, to say something that is vital to me. I use myth and mythical speech because I need it. Anything that is not needed is dead. What drives me to need and to use it?

A first precondition of writing and speaking today is that we protect ourselves from the embrace of the media and keep ourselves free from their rules. These rules dominate our thinking and destroy our ability to hope or (to put it in biblical terms) to see the world through Jesus' eyes. We are not in a position to "see" the woman who brings the tea in the night, to "see" in the sense of *idou*, "take a look," as John the evangelist uses the word. The fact that a woman whose name I do not know brings tea during the night to a group of blockaders is not "news." My attitude—in this case, my joy—is not newsworthy. If I tried to tell the story to a newspaperman, he would think I was crazy, sentimental, off the point—in other words, typically feminine.

My story is unimportant, it says nothing to him or, he thinks, to most people. It is trivial.

The media under whose sway we live and through which we perceive reality make a selection that is always ahead of us and always more powerful than we can "see." The china that Nancy Reagan purchased in Washington for her husband's inauguration is important; the tea that a woman brings us in Mutlangen is unimportant. Inasmuch as the media make a certain selection between "important" and "trivial" things, they incapacitate us and teach us to regard our own lives as trivial, uninteresting, and inessential. In the face of these compulsions, myth—a story that constantly interprets the world as existing in relationship to God—is a help to us. It recalls for us that our story, also, can be told differently, that we, too, live in another relationship to the world than the lords of our consciousness imagine. "Star" does not always mean a heavenly body when the people that walk in darkness see "a great light."

The mythical-narrative language of the Bible parries the pressures of the media and criticizes one of their fundamental presuppositions, that of absolute faith in power and success. One of the messages we receive from the media (and in the United States, young people now watch television an average of six hours a day) is that only success counts. I want to illustrate that with an experience I have had in recent years in connection with the peace movement.

I have given many interviews to all sorts of media people. It took me a long time before I really understood the mechanisms that controlled the process. I unconsciously assumed that in an interview, the interviewer and the interviewee had a shared interest in getting to the truth. This was a naive assumption. What usually interested the reporter was not the truth—for example, whether it was a question of first-strike or defensive weapons, of anticipating or following an escalation in armaments, of the slaughter of Nicaragua or the protection of the Indians' human rights. The principal interest of the media people is to find out whether the peace movement is successful, whether its representatives—I, for example—project power.

The basic cynicism of the media consists in the arrogance of power that they themselves share. How often have they given us to understand that we are certainly "very nice" but pitifully weak? When I attempt to represent the peace movement in such discussions, I first have to try to break through this barrier of the success mentality within which my opposite number lives, to dissolve this obsession with power so that the question of truth can be approached at all. I have to try to achieve a reversal of the priorities of success versus truth before I can make the subject audible at all.

The compulsion to think in terms of success and power, however, touches not only those who work in the media, but all of us. Our ability to perceive has been disturbed and our feeling for reality trivialized. In a culture that expects all of us to be informed daily and hourly about cat food and hair spray, life is necessarily trivial. What this daily brainwashing produces, and what is consumed at particular times and under particular circumstances (news program, sports, beer), have become, in a new sense of the term, our daily ritual, which has replaced the old myths. Just as the planning of a city neighborhood can give a child the message "Cars are important here; you are not wanted," so our means of communication teach all of us a constant, self-evident contempt for living things, the weak, and those in need of protection. What cannot be sold is worthless. What is not immediately successful can be as true as you like, but it won't make it into the TV programs. And the sacredness of life for which I am here trying to plead is consistently and pitilessly destroyed in the rituals of consumerism.

The old myth is a story about life as sacred. This sacredness has to be dramatized again and again so that we do not forget it or think of it as superfluous. In mythical language we give thanks for the sun, bless bread, wish each other a good trip home, and thus recall that life is a gift, not a possession. The woman who brought us tea and the woman with the two copper coins together represent such a dramatization. The remembered myth helps me to combat trivialization.

As a writer I do not want to spend my whole life with words; at some point I want to get to the Word. Writing means for me that I continue the writing of the Bible, going on with the writing of the Book. I want to find the Word of God, to use an often misunderstood and objectivized traditional expression. I am thinking of the Word of God not in terms of its origins, such as that God spoke to people once upon a time two thousand years ago, but in terms of its goal. The Word of God is the word, spoken or unspoken, that shares life and roots us in the Ground of all life. The Word of God is life-giving, life-sharing—whoever utters it. It is not the author who defines the word, as authoritarian neoorthodox Protestantism thinks, but it is the relationship between speaker and hearer that justifies our determining such a word-event to be Word of God. It liberates: there is no other definition of the Word of God.

Meister Eckhart says: "Yet God says: 'No one is good but God alone.' What is good? That which shares itself. We say that a good person is one who shares him- or herself and is of use to others. Thus a heathen scholar says that a hermit is neither good nor bad in this sense, because he neither shares himself with others nor is useful to them. But God is all-sharing."[1]

How shall I express the fact that the poor woman's tea in that rainy night in Mutlangen was "all-sharing," if I restrict my language to that of explanation, definition, and criticism (in the comprehensive Western understanding of that word)? I need more.

Religion expresses itself at three different levels of language: mythical-narrative, religious-confessional, and argumentative-reflective. For example, the phenomenon of human suffering and the deficiency and finitude of life are dealt with religiously in different ways: by telling the myth of Paradise and the banishment of the first humans; by subjective appropriation of our destiny and expression of it in the religious concept of sin; by theological-philosophical reflection on the human situation and attempts to describe it—for example, in the dogma of original sin or its modern derivative, the idea of unchangeable inherited aggressivity. Telling a story, confessing a creed, or constructing a concept are very different forms of religious interpretation of the world. We call them respectively myth, religion, and theology. For secularized consciousness these inner-religious distinctions are rather irrelevant. The three concepts are often used in undifferentiated and pejorative fashion, and popular atheism is right to do so, insofar as it is a matter of different language games about the same thing.

The tradition of religious criticism derived from the Enlightenment takes a position, in face of these three forms of language, that involves faith in progress and an historicizing approach. It is convinced that it can establish an irreversible development, over time, from myth to reason—from mythos to logos. Logos, as the stage of advanced consciousness, has made myth superfluous by "raising it to the level of concepts."

But is this idea of a diachronic process, in which myth passes through religion into logos, a correct description? There are good reasons today to contest the thesis of progressive secularization. In spite of enlightened thought, religion has not made itself superfluous, nor has it become irrelevant for people's life decisions.

It seems to me that we come nearer to the truth of religious consciousness if we regard it synchronically as participating simultaneously in the three different forms of religious expression. My thesis would be: Contemporary, that is, post-Enlightenment, theology must share in all three levels of religious language. Without the narrative element, by which I mean the retelling of the myth and the narrating of my own experience, theology dries up. At the same time it masculinizes itself in a life-threatening absolute sexism. By this I do not only mean that women have nothing to say in this theology and therefore have to be discriminated against institutionally and in print, but also that the theological method of shaping the world in masculine categories makes narrative superfluous. Narrative is, so to speak, superfluous from the start; to put it another way, it is raped from the start into a concept.

The sexism of the theology that dominates both church and university consists not only in the unconscious notion that the human being is a man, but also in an extermination of the mythical-narrative element that has gone far beyond Bultmann's program of demythologization. Bultmann opposed the frozen, cosmic-explanatory myth that had become a fetish in a situation where better explanations were available. But he did it for the sake of the existentially affected truth that disappears and becomes inexpressible in rational-argumentative discourse. Bultmann had learned from Kierkegaard that the "leap" away from the level of reflective consciousness is necessary to faith. In the "leap," myth and prayer recover their voices in religious discourse. Kierkegaard is such a wonderful theologian, in my view, because he speaks all three languages of religion with the passion of the absolute. He tells, he prays, he argues. He does not allow himself to be reduced to one level of language, such as that of ironic reflection.

Great theology has always practiced narrative and prayer; it participates in all three levels of religious discourse. This can be traced as far as Barmen (1934) or Stuttgart (1947). To find contrary examples, one need only read the declarations of the German Lutheran church on the peace question nowadays; there one can comprehend the self-destruction practiced by this theology. It is unable to express either the myth or its religious appropriation. It allows itself to be reduced to a rational mode of reflection in which the aptitude for truth has long since been replaced by an aptitude for consensus. It is a language that increasingly excludes narrative and confessional speech; it has cleansed itself of every form of doubt or other emotion, and it uses theological terminology in a purely instrumental manner. It does not express the sacredness of life, but instead acts like a protective mechanism. Not a word transcends the technocratic language game.

Successful theology, on the contrary, invites the return of the myth. Its language form, that of narrative, is sought for, not banned as impure. That is, incidentally, a criterion of liberation theology, whether black, feminist, or from the viewpoint of the poor. Narration is everywhere: witnesses and storytellers appear at the great ecumenical conferences. When Domitila, the Bolivian woman from the mining district, tells about the hunger strike of four Bolivian housewives, that is what she does—telling and imploring, pleading and accusing, analyzing and reflecting. What she says cannot be set down in a summary. Prayer and narrative defy this form of communication. It freezes them to death.

Today a new synthesis of myth, religion, and reflection is coming to life wherever theology has a liberating character. There the myth is not artificially protected from the clutches of the logos, as orthodoxy tried to do. Instead, it is criticized wherever it legitimizes the domination of some people over others, as in the cases of sexism or racism. The myth is not destroyed for us if we see through the way it functions in a particular situation.

Myth is not made superfluous by the logos. Instead, it is made effective, celebrated, retold. The strongest witnesses of liberation theology are prayers, liturgies, worship plans in which the Christian myth, especially the exodus and the resurrection, is dramatized. That can only happen in groups that are dedicated to changing the world and who do not distance themselves from such an enterprise by withdrawing into academic resignation. They need God because the general interpretation of "this world," which controls them, is a death sentence for the poor: they must become poorer so that the rich can become richer. It is an illusion to suppose that we live in a world that can be understood and controlled by science and that can do without such interpretive categories as a God who is justice. Only the rich can conveniently live without God.

The return of myth is happening among those who need its hope. That is the foundation of what is called, in liberation theology, the teaching office of the poor. From the poor we learn the contrast-language of hope.

Note

1. Meister Eckhart, *Deutsche Predigten und Traktate* (Munich: C. Hanser, 1955), Sermon 26, 197. He uses the German term *Allermit-teilsamste*.